Hi Max – Good to hear from you!
Enjoy Our Wilderness!
Keep Healthy!
Clayton Klein

Cold Summer Wind II

by Clayton Klein

Wilderness Adventure Books
Manchester, Michigan

Unless otherwise indicated, all photographs taken by Clayton, Darrell, or Debbie Klein

Front Cover: *Darrell Klein on Putahow Lake*
Back Cover: *Photo courtesy of Akitoshi Nishimura*
Maps by: *Erin Bardsley, Marjorie Nash Klein*

ISBN: 0-923568-49-2

Wilderness Adventure Books
P.O. Box 856
Manchester, MI 48158

Printed in the United States of America

To my canoeing adventure partners

Darrell Klein

Deborah Klein

and

to Marjorie Nash Klein, who waited, prayed

and worried at home while we three

explored and enjoyed America's Northern Wilderness.

Acknowledgments

Cold Summer Wind II became a reality because of the cooperation and suggestions of these people:

Special thanks to Ronald Craven for his assistance in locating Ilse Schweder Clements.

Particular thanks to Bryan and Ilse Clements for providing the photo and correct details of The Rescue.

Definite thanks to R. King Pettigrew for his cooperation and permission to use his chapter, "Ragnar's Wolverine" from his wonderful book, ***North of Stony Rapids.***

Personal thanks to Gerry Dunning for his permission to use much of a chapter from his book, ***When the Foxes Ran***, about the life of Charles Schweder and Windy River Post.

Special thanks to Gordon Wallace and his staff at Selwyn Lake Lodge and to guides John Louis Youya, Billy Joe Mercredi, Chief Leon Cook and Pierre Broussie for their assistance.

Thanks to Bob Voss, whose conversations certainly added to our exploration in north central Canada.

Lynda Holland & Bill Layman of LaRonge for their helpful suggestions and maps of the area west of Nueltin Lake.

Chris Rayner for assistance with keyboarding the manuscript and other computer duties.

Table of Contents

List of Illustrations

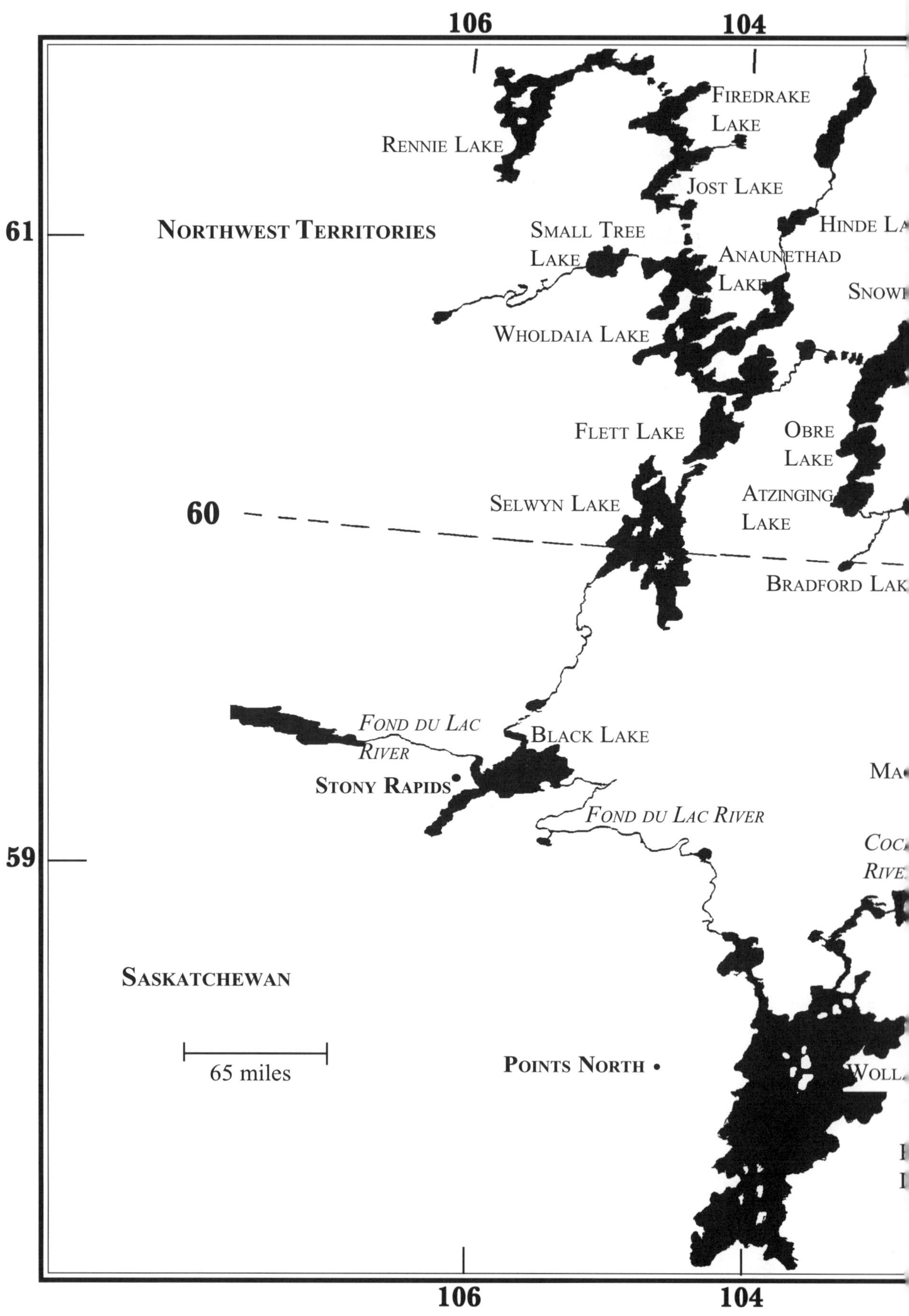
106
104
61
59
60
Firedrake Lake
Rennie Lake
Jost Lake
Northwest Territories
Small Tree Lake
Hinde La
Anaunethad Lake
Snowi
Wholdaia Lake
Flett Lake
Obre Lake
Atzinging Lake
Selwyn Lake
Bradford Lak
Fond du Lac River
Black Lake
Stony Rapids
Ma
Fond du Lac River
Coc
Rive
Saskatchewan
65 miles
Points North
Woll
106
104

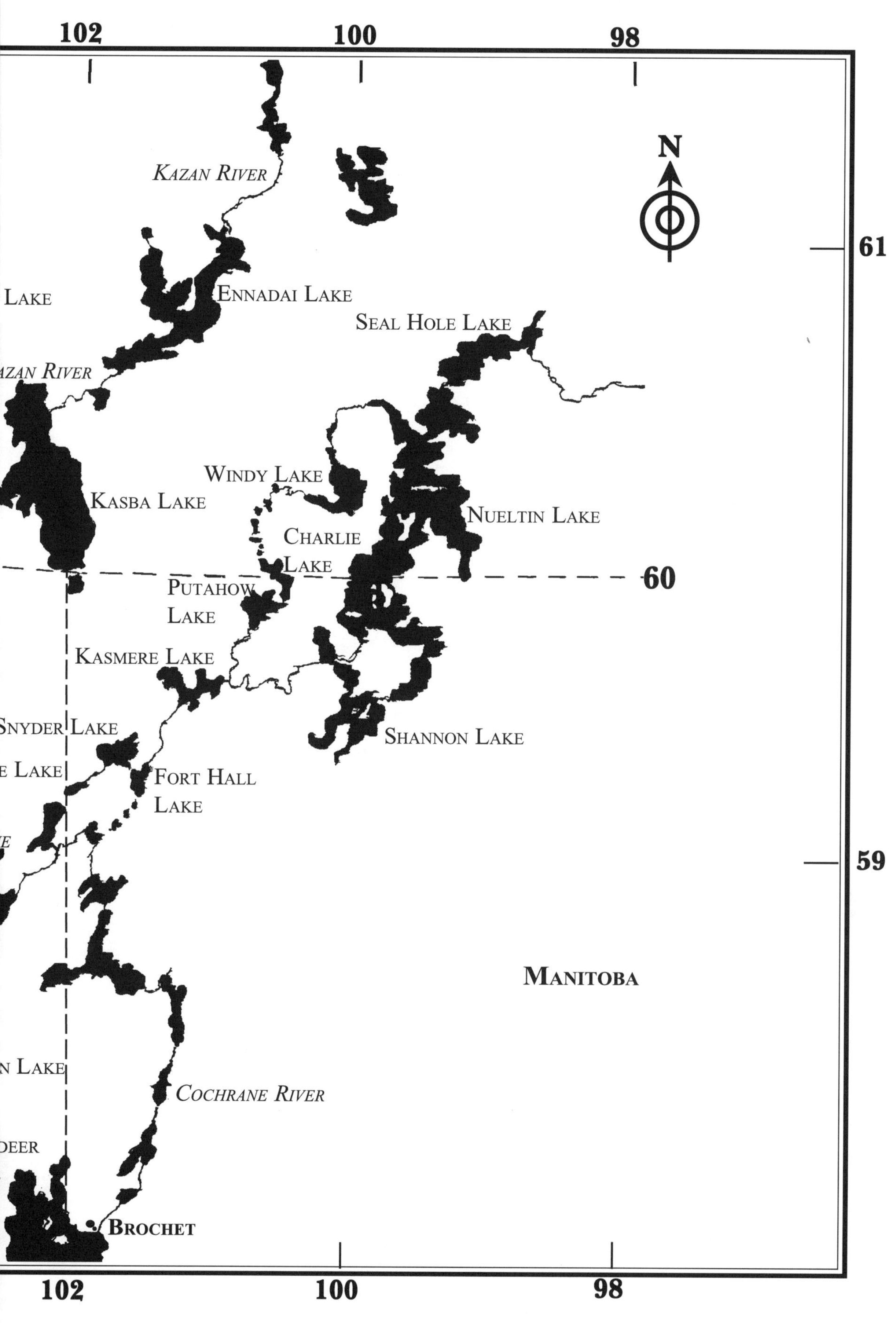
102
100
98
N
Kazan River
Ennadai Lake
Lake
Seal Hole Lake
61
Windy Lake
Kasba Lake
Nueltin Lake
Charlie
Lake
60
Putahow
Lake
Kasmere Lake
Snyder Lake
Shannon Lake
Fort Hall
Lake
59
Manitoba
Cochrane River
Brochet
102
100
98

Other Books by Clayton Klein

Cold Summer Wind	1983
One Incredible Journey	1985
A Passion For Wilderness	1986
Challenge the Wilderness	1988
Campfire Poems	1995

There's a race of men that don't fit in,
A race that can't stay still;
So they break the hearts of kith and ken,
And they roam the world at will.
—Robert W. Service

Introduction

Many people enjoy nature and have a built-in desire to learn more about things wild and free. Most are born with an inherent passion for wilderness and often seek out those natural places that are undisturbed by people and their machines.

A few of us, when thinking or speaking of wilderness, mean what is often referred to as "true wilderness." True wilderness is a roadless area well out of reach of any type of motorized conveyance other than the occasional aircraft. To visit true wilderness, one usually paddles a canoe or kayak after flying or backpacking in.

When people first traveled in North America, they followed streams and rivers. These arteries thus became the original highways of the continent. This is what ***Cold Summer Wind II*** is all about. We have paddled numerous rivers and waterways in northern Canada. In doing so we satisfied our immense desire to get off the beaten path and experience nature first-hand in real wilderness settings. This volume begins with our search for and days spent with Master of the Wilderness, Ragnar Jonsson.

Then we move to the north of Great Bear Lake as we descend the Ross and Anderson Rivers down to the Arctic Ocean. Then comes the Lockhart River and north shore of Great Slave Lake. Other river highways traveled were the Yukon from Whitehorse to Circle, Alaska followed by explorations in the upper reaches of the Thelon, Dubuant and Kazan watersheds.

A major discovery was the Sacred Lake and Holy Mountain of the Chipewyan Indians. Then there is our search for the secret Japanese communications setup that was thought to be established during World War II in central Canada.

You are invited to bring your paddle and join us as the Cessna on floats and splashes down on the surface of Maguire Lake in the headwaters of the Thlewiaza River in Northwest Territories. As we move along you will experience the true wilderness, learning about trapping and the history of the fur trade in the early years of the twentieth century as told by our hermit of the north, Ragnar Jonsson and his friend Charles Schweder.

1

The Search Begins

Flying a Cessna 185, the Parson's Airways pilot put us ashore on an island in southwestern Maguire Lake. Stepping ashore, fresh bear tracks along the beach reaffirmed the fact that we had once again returned to the wilderness. As a precautionary measure we placed our dry box of food and packs alongside the tent and later turned the canoe upside down over them.

Enjoying our first campsite, after supper we paddled around our island, then built a beach fire before calling it a day just before midnight. The bear gave us no problems, however, the next morning another set of fresh tracks by the same animal were on the beach. This time the bruin had stopped short of our tent by fourteen paces before eventually turning back into the bush.

It was early in August of 1981 when my daughter Debbie and I flew from Lynn Lake, Manitoba north to Maguire Lake in the headwaters of the Thlewiaza River. We were going in search of the legendary trapper Ragnar Jonsson. We had been told he might be camping somewhere along the Thlewiaza. Our goal was to find Mr. Jonsson, do an interview and get some photos. There was no question his life story would make good reading. For those who have not read ***Cold Summer Wind***, the following quote gives a brief introduction to this "hermit of the north."

> Ragnar Jonsson is the man we heard about while in Brochet in 1964. He only comes south to Brochet once each five years to pick up his mail and trade at the Hudson's Bay post. While we were there that summer, the post manager told us they were expecting Mr. Jonsson to arrive soon as it had been five years since he last came down to pick up his mail. There were several boxes of mail waiting for him at the post.
>
> The Bay manager had told us that the old fellow roams around somewhere up in Northwest Territories with his dogs and does some trapping. He said when Mr. Jonsson came to pick up his mail in 1946, people were still talking about the war. Finally Mr. Jonsson asked why they were discussing the war, as it had been twenty-eight years since the war had ended. They told him that there had been another World War. That was the first time he had heard anything about WWII as he had been out of contact with civilization since picking up his mail in 1941.

There was a second reason we chose the Thlewiaza. I was eager to have Debbie see the old abandoned trading post known as Fort Hall and to travel along the Old North Trail between the Cochrane River and Fort Hall Lake. We would end our travels in Lovell Lake, the southernmost of the little lakes along the Old North Trail and only a half-mile east of the Cochrane River.

With nearly perfect canoeing weather the next morning we headed to the lake's outlet and downstream. By mid-afternoon we had made a couple of sweaty portages in the 82° temperature and entered Kilpatrick Lake. Then, crossing Snyder Lake with a huge forest fire burning along its western shore, it was on down the Thlewiaza into Hillhouse Lake.

Loons were plentiful all along the way, frequently serenading us as we paddled along. At times they would come in close to look us over before slowly sink-diving out of site. Camping along the east shore of Hillhouse, after going for a swim, we watched and listened as three common loons sang their songs of sweet music. Earlier we had recorded several loon songs on our little tape recorder. During the evening we enjoyed playing the tape for those intelligent birds. They showed a lot of interest and curiosity moving in close to shore as they listened. A few minutes later they were joined by another loon family and together, following a loon chat, the entire group moved out on the lake and danced on the surface for us.

Moving on downstream, we crossed Layton Lake in rainy weather, making only one portage before arriving in Fort Hall Lake. There, in the southwestern bay while heading for an old abandoned log cabin, we stopped to pick up some fish net floats on the surface. Picking one up we discovered it was attached to an old rotting net, which had been left in the lake for many months or years. We attempted to lift the net. What a mess! Dozens of fish had died there after being caught in the deteriorating mash.

During the afternoon, while paddling to the northeast on Fort Hall Lake, a thunderstorm rolled toward us. We rushed to get ashore on the esker we could see ahead. Arriving just before the storm, we quickly erected the tent above a beach on the right, only to then observe the downpour was passing by less than a quarter mile to the south. We were at the narrows of the lake, opposite the peninsula extending into the lake from the western shore. This was the exact spot where I had camped in 1968 while traveling from Snowbird Lake to Brochet, Manitoba with Darrell, Bryan Beasley and Loren Jonckheere.

The sun was soon dimly shining again even though red in color as it shone through the dense smoke of the nearby burning forest. Following a swim off the sand beach, we walked along above the esker's high cut-banks face. "When the four of us came through here in '68," I told Debbie, "the tip of the peninsula over there was covered with pens and a big corral of poles. Some are still visible. This had to have been a caribou crossing place. The Canadian game management people likely used the corral and pens in their study of the barren land caribou that winter in the forests of this area."

We soon came to a wooden cross still standing plus two others lying flat on

The remains of Chief Kasmere's grave in 2001

the ground near the face of the cut-bank. "One of these must be the grave of old Chief Kasmere," I said, recalling my reading of the book ***Sleeping Island*** by P.G. Downes. "Mr. Downes paddled up through here in the summer of 1939. There were still many Chipewyans using this waterway at the time and one of those Downes met was Chief Kasmere. He wrote that 'Kasmere was a very old man, still broad, squat and powerful looking.'"

"That's interesting," Debbie replied.

"The old fellow is most likely standing right down there," I continued while pointing at the earth beneath the cross, "as I recall, Downes wrote that Kasmere had said to a member of his band, 'When I die, bury me standing up. Bury me high on the hill at the narrows, and there I shall stand and watch you, my people, as you go north to hunt the deer. I will see you all as you pass and will wish you luck in the killing of the deer.'"

Standing there reverently reflecting, I continued, "The old fellow was the chief of the Barren Land Band and was the dominating personality of this area for decades. In fact, when Ernest Oberholtzer and Billy Magee came through here in 1912, they found a conical lookout tower of spruce trees on this hilltop. From up here Chief Kasmere could see the country for miles in any direction."

We enjoyed our camp at the narrows and decided to leave the tent standing there for another night. In the meantime we would paddle the eleven miles down to the old trading post in Thanout Lake.

Debbie Klein at Fort Hall in 1981

The abandoned building along the west shore of the lake looked very lonely standing there in the clearing as we arrived about mid-day. We found it to be much the way I remembered it as the four of us passed it in 1968. The major difference was one large section of the roof had since collapsed. There were clumps of fireweed in full bloom and some old graves nearby. As we walked around with cameras in hand while munching on ripe red raspberries, Debbie asked, "Do you have any idea about how long this place has been here?"

"Yes. As I recall from reading ***Sleeping Island***, it was built in 1908 by an independent trader named Herbert Hall who worked closely with the Hudson's Bay Company. The location here was most likely a good one as they traded goods for furs with both the Inuit from the north and also the Chipewyans. I remember reading an article by R.H. Cockburn in *The Beaver* that this place was operated by the HBC until sometime in the 1920s."

When a strong southwest wind suddenly whipped up, we changed our plan for the day. Instead of paddling the final mile down to Kasmere Falls, we decided to head back to our camp at the narrows. "It's too bad we didn't bring our tent along. We could have camped right here by the post," Deb said as we paddled away.

I agreed. After five hours of nosing directly into the wind we made it back to our campsite just beyond Chief Kasmere's grave. We had found no signs of Ragnar Jonsson but there was still a slim chance we might intercept him along the Old North Trail if this happened to be his year to make a trip to Brochet.

The next morning we broke camp heading southwest toward the trail. With three days remaining before our pickup date in Lovell Lake there was no reason to rush. I recalled from our journey in '68, the four of us had covered the entire trail through its eight little lakes to the Cochrane River in one long day. This time we made it into Smith-House Lake the first day. Most of the time smoke from the forest fires to the west completely obscured the sun. When it did peek through, it looked like a dim red ball in the sky.

The scenery was a thing of beauty as we crossed sandy-bottomed Blue Lake with its large spruce trees growing along the slope of an esker along the lake's western shore. Then we moved on over the trail's steep and now little used portages through Ratinsky, Wolf Island and the other smaller lakes. We arrived in Lovell on August 12 and were flown back to Lynn Lake the following morning.

We had found no trace of Ragnar Jonsson. We had seen no other person along the way. Asking our pilot about Mr. Jonsson, his reply was, "Yes. I've heard about the old fellow. I think he's somewhere up around Wholdaia Lake in Northwest Territories."

So, we had been looking in the incorrect river system! But, even so, it had been a memorable trip.

2

(ellow Eyes

rrived, both Debbie and I were ready to continue our sson. This time we had secured a new eighteen-foot nodel canoe, weighing only sixty pounds. We thought o handle both on the portages and in the water.

nents for a flight from Wollaston Lake in Saskatchewan Territories by Eagle Airways. We would get to drive north of Lac La Ronge to Wollaston Lake Lodge on e thought, the people at Eagle Air or at the Lodge we could find Mr. Jonsson. To our dismay, no one at knew anything about him. Disappointed at this news, n as planned. "We may be on another 'wild goose go and have a look anyway. Maybe we'll get lucky."

pilot Les Barker at the controls of a Cessna 185, our aft's right pontoon loosened and was about ready to fall off. He made an emergency landing in a small lake north of the Fon du Lac River. Once better secured we were soon airborne again. An hour later we were dropped off in the center of southern Flett Lake. Before the Cessna departed, we asked to be picked up along the western shore of Flett nine days later.

With high country on both sides of the lake we paddled to the west shore and soon found a suitable campsite on a little peninsula jutting out toward a small island. The next morning, with a strong breeze out of the southeast, we paddled to the east shore following it and several islands to the north. By mid-afternoon we arrived at an esker opposite the north tip of the lake's largest island. The weather looked like rain so we set up camp on the softly carpeted esker top.

The rains moved in and continued until after sunset. Strong winds continued the next day so we stayed put. Walking along the esker with rod in hand, we found a small lake a mile or so away and tried to catch a fish for supper. Approaching the little lake a solitary sandpiper spotted us and instantly began spreading the alarm as it flew near us and soon landed on a branch near the top of a black spruce. Geese went scurrying away from our side of the lake calling for their goslings to follow. Other small shore birds flew away as the sandpiper continued its shrill and voluptuous incessant cry.

We caught no fish but would survive as we had packed in ample food for more than two weeks. Returning to camp we found our Gerry Fortnight II tent had collapsed in the near gale force winds. We set it up again in a more protected place with tent the facing directly into the wind. Then, while Debbie began laying plans for a pancake supper, I walked back to the small lake with my camera and tape recorder. I wanted to capture the loud and unending *weet-weet-weet-weet* of the solitary sandpiper. I was not disappointed. The bird performed perfectly as anticipated, continuing as long as I remained in the vicinity.

Returning from the little lake, I had an unexpected surprise. Walking along the slope of the esker, I came upon a wolf den. There were fresh tracks all over the mound of sand out front. Wanting to look down into the entrance, I was less than fifteen feet away when a big white wolf came charging out of the den. She turned and ran a couple or three jumps to the side, abruptly stopped, and half turned to look at me. I froze, standing perfectly still, looking into her large yellow eyes. Then speaking slowly in as friendly a voice as I could muster "Hi there doggy, Hi doggy, Hi doggy." She stood staring at me for more than a minute. It would have made the perfect photo of a tundra wolf. My camera was hanging on a strap around my neck. Slowly I raised my hand to move the camera into position. But as my hand began to move, she had seen enough and away she ran. Ten minutes later I was telling Debbie about it as we enjoyed our pancake supper.

The wind had completely died by the next morning. Before breaking camp we both walked back to the wolf den hoping to see some action. No wolves were in sight so we looked into the tunnel entrance and could see about twelve feet back and down but no animals were there. A piece of caribou bone with a trace of red meat on it, plus more fresh tracks on the sandy mound in front of the den, showed there had been plenty of action overnight.

Paddling to the north end of Flett, we had difficulty locating the half-mile

Tundra wolf—but not Yellow Eyes

portage over into Wholdaia Lake. Eventually we stumbled onto it and moved across by mid-afternoon. There were no signs of anyone else crossing the trail since the previous winter. We were still hoping to find someone, somewhere who could tell us where we might find Mr. Jonsson.

We moved along the shores and islands of Wholdaia Lake for the next eight days looking for any clue of his whereabouts. Finally, along the north shore of the bay leading to the outlet of Lone Lake, we came upon a log cabin with teepees standing nearby. With high hopes we put ashore. Could this be Mr. Jonsson's base camp or did it belong to a Chipewyan family? Soon, we discovered there were no people or dogs currently living there. We walked around looking things over. There were three outbound motors, a large boat and a freighter canoe. There were several stakes where sled dogs had been tied and it was obvious the dogs had been fed both fish and caribou. There were lots of caribou skins lying around, as well as a white wolf head, a moose head and the complete bones of the hindquarter of a moose. It was apparent; whoever the place belonged to had been gone for most of the summer.

Moving on to the east and south we enjoyed watching still more wildlife including moose, swans, eagles, loons and a myriad of shorebirds. Nearing the end of the journey while camping along the east arm of Flett Lake, just above the outlet, we had caught another jackfish for supper. The shore below our camp was weedy, so to dip a bucket of fresh water I sat on the stern seat of the canoe while Debbie remained on shore with the bow rope in her hand. I pushed with the paddle back and out into the deep water, leaned over dipping the bucket full. Then "OK, pull" I said. She did and instantly the canoe flipped over and into Flett Lake I went. I came up with my hat floating on the surface but I also waded ashore with a bucket full of fresh water. We both had some good laughs about it as I put on dry pants and shirt after dumping water from my boots.

We were more than a day ahead of schedule so the next day we decided to walk west on the esker and have another look at the wolf den. A strong wind was blowing from the southeast and insects were no major problem. On our walk to the den we found an abandoned Chipewyan village with one log cabin still standing. At one time in the past there had been more than a half dozen others. It was an interesting 2 miles to the den, open and park-like with many large rocks on the esker surface. Approaching the den quietly and cautiously we were disappointed to see no wolves. There were many more fresh tracks, mostly made by the pups. On our return toward the canoe we photographed one huge rock roughly 25 feet square and standing at least 20 feet high that had been left on the esker's surface by the melting glacier.

The final twenty miles to our pickup in Flett's southwest corner was a struggle into near gale force winds from the southeast. Whenever possible we hugged the east shore or cut downwind of several of the islands. The Wenonah we were using was difficult to control while broadsiding a strong wind in heavy breaking waves. Crossing bays in open water we were crabbing to the left by 40 or 50 degrees to follow a direct line to the next downwind point of the nearest shore. It was a struggle and a little scary at times but we made it back to our first camping place in time to be picked up on the fourth of August.

Once more we had found no trace of Ragnar Jonsson nor had we seen any other people in the entire area. It had indeed turned out to have been another wild goose chase, though an enjoyable camping experience for the two of us.

3

Master of the Wilderness

A news item and photo of trapper Ragnar Jonsson appeared in our daily newspaper, the *Lansing State Journal,* on October 3, 1982. He was in a Winnipeg hospital. The (AP) news story said he needed cataract surgery on his right eye, his 'shooting eye.' This was the first time he had been south as far as Winnipeg since he first arrived in Canada in 1923.

Good news! Immediately I picked up the telephone and called the hospital. Inquiring about Mr. Jonsson, I learned he had left the hospital the day before. Then I asked if they knew where he was staying in Winnipeg. The nurse responded, "Oh! I think he has already gone back up north. He just couldn't wait to get out of the city. He told me, 'There's so many people around here and they all seem to be in such a horrible hurry to get somewhere.'"

Early in 1983 I called Parson's Airways Northern and spoke with Robert G. Ferguson in FlinFlon, Manitoba. When I inquired about Mr. Jonsson, Mr. Ferguson told me they were now frequently in touch with Ragnar. He volunteered to deliver a letter from me. So the letter was sent. In June, calling Mr. Ferguson again, I learned that Ragnar was doing fine, was at his camp on Windy River in Northwest Territories and he would like to have me come for a visit.

With canoe and camping gear, daughter Debbie and I arrived in Lynn Lake on July 18. The Parsons Airways people were ready for us. George Friesen told us they had been in contact with Ragnar and he would be waiting for us at Nueltin Lakes Tree Line Lodge.

We were unloading the plane after arrival at the Tree Line dock when I noticed an elderly man leaning against an upturned fifty-five gallon fuel drum on the nearby beach. Walking over to him I said, "Ragnar Jonsson, is this you?"

"Yes." He responded with a smile, reaching out to shake my hand, "I'm glad you came to see me." Introductions were soon completed and we proceeded up the esker toward the sign, which read, Welcome to Tree Line Lodge. Ragnar invited us into his nearby tent where we chatted for awhile. I was soon telling him about our searches for him and just how we managed to track him down. Then I asked, "Did the eye surgery really improve your vision?"

"Oh! Yes. Now I can read again. I've always enjoyed reading."

"Glad to hear it." Then I asked, reaching into my side pocket, "Is it all right with you if I turn on this little tape recorder? I do want to be sure to get everything correct when I write up the things you have to say."

"That's fine," he nodded affirmatively, brushing away some mosquitoes.

The mosquitoes were also feasting on Debbie and me, so we took a short break as Deb pulled some Off from her pack that we passed around. Then I asked, "Ragnar, tell us a little about yourself. How long have you been up here, and also tell us about your earlier life."

"I've been here around Nueltin Lake since 1939. I like it up here. Not as crowded with people," he grinned. "I grew up on a farm near Ornskoldsvik, Sweden and came to Canada in 1923, the year I turned twenty-three. Wanting to see the country, I rode the train all the way to B.C. I soon found work on a farm near Mission. A few months later I got a job with a work crew on the railroad and was soon transferred back east to Regina. Then I decided that I wanted to see the north and eventually made my way up to Big River, northwest of Prince Albert."

"When did you begin trapping?" I asked.

"It was while I was in Big River," he chuckled and his blue eyes sparkled. "There were a lot of pine martins, beaver, muskrat, otters, mink and other animals around there. Fur prices were good. I did good during those years. But then I decided to see more of the country so I went over to Ile La Crosse. Only stayed there one season. There were too many people there. Then I went to Stony Rapids. You know where that is?"

"Sure. On the Fon du Lac River."

"That's right. I found a nice place to stay there. Stayed three years. Some nice people in Stony. Had lotsa fun while I was there." He grinned, "Then I trap up around High Rock Lake."

Ragner visits our camp

"You did move around a lot. Of course you traveled by dog teams in the winter-time."

"Dogs? No. In those days I didn't need dogs. You have to feed dogs," he laughed.

"Then how did you get around to check your traps?"

"Skis. I used Lapp skis. So you know what they are?"

"No," I replied. "Debbie skis. Do you know what they are, Deb?"

"No, I don't."

"They are about eight or ten inches wide," Ragnar explained, motioning with his hands, "and around six feet long, curved up in front and they have a deep grove about an inch wide cut in the bottom. You can move right along on them and they don't slip sideways. I carried my supplies in a pack-sack on my back with a tump-line. Lapp skis are wonderful! Just wonderful!"

"You must have had snowshoes too?"

"Yeah. I had snowshoes for a while but seldom used 'em. I bought my first dog team in 1934. I had been at Wollaston Lake for six years. Made good money there even during the Depression. Trapping was sure good to me. That's when I bought my first dogs. Four of 'em. I skied over to Fort Chipewyan and bought 'em. Do you know where that is?"

"Yes. That's over near the west end of Lake Athabaska. It's a long ways from Wollaston."

"Yeah. Then I went over to Reindeer Lake near Brochet until I came up here in 1939," he paused.

Then I cut in, asking where we could set up our tent well away from the Lodge. He told us about a big sand beach about a mile to the north. Ragnar was currently having his meals at Tree Line. We told him we would get our camp set and return in the evening.

Two hours later we heard a motor boat coming around the point. It was Ragnar and a guide from the lodge. Ragnar wanted to see our camp and we soon learned he would also like to try out our Voyageur canoe. The guide shoved off and headed back to the Lodge when I assured him we would paddle with Ragnar back to his tent a little while later. A good breeze had been holding the insects at bay so the three of us enjoyed tea and cookies as we chatted. He asked for some sugar for his tea but we had none with us.

I asked him to tell us about his early days at Nueltin and also to tell us about some of the people he used to know around the lake.

"Well," he responded, "the first season I found some Chips (Chipewyans) along the west side of the lake. There were lots of animals around here to catch in those days and caribou. Those caribou passed through here by the thousands every spring and fall," he paused.

"Were there quite a few Chipewyans around Nueltin Lake back then?"

"This used to be the capital of the Chips. Yeah! You'd see them all over the place! And caribou! The Chips and white trappers killed caribou by the thousands around here and all the way down to Reindeer Lake. The Chips killed them for food and their skins you see. But they shot many more than they could use. Thousands more every year! Horrid! And that's true! Just like now, men kill the baby seals in Newfoundland."

"They really didn't think they were likely going to kill them nearly all off," I replied. "It must have been similar to the way our people nearly wiped out all of the bison in the 1800s. I understand the caribou are now beginning to make a comeback. Is that true?"

"They're starting to make a comeback, yes. You see there are also less white trappers in the barren lands than there used to be. They used to go out for white foxes, you see, and they shot caribou for bait for their traps."

"Oh! They did?"

"Yes. That's what they did. They shot them by the hundreds."

"Are foxes still plentiful around here?"

"Not any more. They used to be. The first years I was here were the best. Foxes were still quite plentiful then and prices were good. By the early '50s foxes were getting scarce and prices low. Some years even the white foxes brought only $5.00 and the colored were worth maybe a dollar."

"I'll bet you've built several log cabins in all the years you've been in the north," I said during a lull in the conversation. With a puzzled look on his face, he asked me to repeat the statement.

"Only one," he replied. "I've had a much more efficient method for shelter."

Thinking he may have been joking, I asked, "What's that?"

"Teepees," he grinned. "Teepees are easy to build. They are easy to heat in cold weather and my teepees are mosquito proof. I now have eight of 'em. My nearest teepee is on an island only about three miles from here. Would you like to see it?"

"We sure would! If tomorrow's weather is good, how would you like to paddle out there and show us around?"

Standing up from where he had been sitting on the bow of the upturned ca-

One of Ragnar's teepees with a smoke stack protruding

noe, Ragnar glanced around at the sky conditions saying, “The weather looks like a few more days of good stuff are coming. Let’s plan on it.” Later in the evening with Ragnar in the bow, we paddled with him back to his tent near the Lodge.

4

Visit With Ragnar

Ragnar had been right. The next morning dawned bright and clear. We picked him up after breakfast and headed north. Our Dry Box made a seat for Debbie. Ragnar paddled with power all the way to his esker island, except while we took a short break. We put ashore on a sandy beach along the southwest side of the island. There were two old boats turned upside down as well as some old fuel drums, an empty bucket, fishnets and several old teepee poles nearby. We followed Ragnar about a hundred yards up the trail into the trees and there stood his teepee. This one was covered with corrugated metal sheets. A red squirrel chattered from a nearby spruce as we looked around. A twenty-gallon oil drum lying alongside the structure was rigged with a stovepipe entering into the side of the teepee. "With a low fire in the drum," he explained, "the smoke passes up the pipe, circulates inside the teepee and out the top making it mosquito proof. In the winter I make a larger fire. Heat comes up the stack and keeps me comfortably warm. When there is plenty of snow, I pile snow against the sides for insulation. I keep plenty warm, even on the coldest nights."

While he was explaining, a pair of chattering whisky jacks (Canadian jays) arrived in the nearby branches of a black spruce. Ragnar spoke, "Here come my birds!" Reaching into his pocket, he pulled out a crust of bread. Holding it out toward them, one of the jays instantly came and landed on Ragnar's wrist and began eating. The other bird raucously scolded for a minute, then joined into the feast as Ragnar stood there smiling and repeating over and over, "My birds, yes. These are my hungry birds."

There was a nice breeze blowing from the west as we moved out of the trees and back to the beach. While listening to the Master of the Wilderness talk of his memories, we were soon seated on the bottom of his old boat and our Dry Box.

"I really like it up here." Shaking his head, "It sure beats the mad hassle I saw last fall when I was in Winnipeg. So dang many, many people! All in such a big hurry to get somewhere! I couldn't live like that! Around here you can start out with fifty cents in your pocket in the fall and still have the same fifty cents in the spring," he grinned.

"I know you want to learn about some of the things I've done in my years up here, I've had some good ones, I'll tell you that. We talked some about this last night, but when I first came to Nueltin there were lots of Chips around here because then there were lots of caribou coming down every year. For instance in 1940, I was up at Nueltin Lake Post. You know where that is?" I nodded affirmatively. "There were hundreds of thousands of deer came down and the Chips just shot them down on the tundra for the foxes and wolves to feed on. That's what they did. And the white fox trappers, they also killed the little fawns for

Ragnar's teepee on Jonsson Island

their skins. Horrible! Those big herds used to come down through here. One fall I was camped up near the Narrows and those deer marched by for two weeks. Yes. Several rows of them for two solid weeks! Now the herds are much smaller and some still come down to winter in the bush towards Reindeer Lake. And the wolves didn't kill them off. No siree! Men did! There were over three million of them in the country when I came up here. The wolves got the blame for it. Yes siree! I used to catch lots of arctic wolves on this lake. I caught fifty-six on this lake in one winter when the government paid me $25.00 per head. I made good money then."

"Are there many wolves around Nueltin Lake now?" I asked.

"No, a few. Just a few. They always come around when the caribou come. And there used to be lots of wolverines, too. But now there are no wolverines around here. Haven't seen one in years."

"I've seen only one wolverine in my life," I replied.

"Yeah! I've caught thirty of 'em in one winter."

"Wow! They tell me wolverines were a nuisance to trappers. Don't they steal the bait from your traps?"

"Yeah. But that doesn't tell all of the story. No siree! They also eat the animals you have caught in your traps before you can get to them. They follow your tracks from the previous trip from trap to trap and destroy the animals before you get back to 'em. The wolverine is easy to catch now that I've learned how. Yes, very easy to catch."

Ragnar went on to explain his method of setting some sticks in a semi-circle and hanging a bait about four feet above the trap. He continued, "The wolverine goes up to take the bait and he walks around on his hind legs. There's nothing to it! And you use a spring pole. When he gets caught, it lifts him up!" He laughed.

"They have the reputation of being tough little animals," I said.

"Yes. They fight to the finish!" He paused and grinned. "Years ago when I was trapping over near High Rock Lake I still hadn't learned the proper way to catch 'em. There was one dang old wolverine gave me a bad time, destroying everything caught in my traps time after time. I spent most of one winter hunting down that wily old devil. But I finally got him!" Ragnar proceeded to relate the story of his trials and tribulations as he hunted down the old troublemaker.

Ragnar Jonsson in the summer of 1983

5

Ragnar's Wolverine

NOTE: This chapter is excerpted from the book ***North of Stony Rapids*** *by R. King Pettigrew of Victoria, B.C. Mr. Pettigrew was a geologist with the Geological Survey of Canada when he met the then young Ragnar Jonsson in Stony Rapids, Saskatchewan. It was the spring of 1938.*

Trappers Hall in Stony served as a Bunkhouse and a meeting place for visitors—Indians and white men alike. The nighttime activities, words and stories told there remain a vivid memory. The camaraderie between this mixed group was something to behold. Laughter often rang around the room.

One trapper, who made it a point to drop in at Trappers Hall whenever visitors from the south were there, was a Swede by the name of Ragnar Jonsson. He had spent years in the north. For the past few years, Ragnar had lived in a small cabin directly across the Fon du Lac River from Stony Rapids. Each evening while we were at Stony, he would motor across the mile width of fast water in his stout canoe. At this time of year the rapids were strong but Ragnar made the crossing look easy. Outsiders were a rare commodity at Stony, and Ragnar loved the association with newcomers. In particular, he enjoyed having fresh and willing listeners around to soak up his stories.

The Swede was a heavyset, barrel-chested man. He bragged about his strength. He was proud of the weight he could carry and his ability as a wrestler. He said he could run for ten miles without stopping while breaking trail ahead of his dog team. He was in the prime of his life and, no doubt, in the peak of condition. The man probably was as tough as he said he was.

And Ragnar was a talker—a storyteller of some renown in these parts. Within minutes of his arrival at Trappers Hall, he took over most of the conversation. As he warmed to his subject his voice would rise, and we would find ourselves caught up in the tall tales of bravado and hunting adventure. We enjoyed listening to his accent and the lilting singsong inflection, so characteristic of the Swedish tongue.

Ragnar's zest and enthusiasm for any activity or any subject was boundless. His shouts of laughter, usually brought on by the colorful descriptions of his own experiences, literally shook Trappers Hall. In wrestling bouts he was a veritable powerhouse. His muscles bulged, his blonde hair flew about, and his pale blue eyes shone with glee. Once victorious, he'd head for the beer-barrel and swig down a pint or so of the fermenting juice—still talking and gesticulating between swallows.

In spinning tales of daring-do, Ragnar moved about constantly. His arms waved, he gestured—he relived the events. He played all the parts, including those of the hunted animal. He sang his own praises without embarrassment when it suited a whopping tale, and he took it for granted that we would believe these yarns—however implausible.

Ragnar was a type who thrived on an audience—it stirred up his actor's blood. Our group, along with a few Indians, was the ideal mix for Ragnar. We listened, we questioned, we laughed and cheered him on. And each evening, late, Ragnar would motor back across the untamed Fon du Lac to his cabin. We would hear his strident voice echoing back to us as we watched him from the shore.

One of Ragnar's stories—he swore it to be true—involved the hunting down of a cagey, wily, brainy and experienced old Wolverine that for years had caused him trouble. The animal had eluded Ragnar's every try to capture him alive or to finish him off with a well-aimed bullet. Persistently, the Beast robbed his traps and fouled his caches of food. It forced its way into the stout log cabin and tore up bedding and equipment.

For three years Ragnar had put up with the wolverine's bedevilment. Periodically he would track him and lay traps and snares. He would tempt him with the choicest of meat. Ragnar tried deadfall traps and springpole traps. He dug deep pits and camouflaged them with elaborate care. Nothing worked. The old Wolverine sprung the traps and tripped the snare wires. The animal urinated on the poisoned meat, circled the pits, and continued to play his dirty, devilish tricks.

The Wolverine directed its animosity against Ragnar's intrusion into its rightful territory. Over the three years of the feud between man and animal, the animal had killed two of Ragnar's Husky dogs and then chewed up the dog harness. More than once it shredded, and then fouled, valuable stores of prize furs. Ragnar tried to make his cabin Wolverine-proof but eventually, using its strength and cunning, the fiend would find a way to get in. It was as though his very Spirit entered through the thick log walls.

On the trapline Ragnar would often see him at a distance. Then, like a wraith, he'd be gone. Often, Ragnar's sixth sense made him look around. Turning, he would find his Old Enemy tracking him! In the dark of many a winter's night Ragnar would hear his dogs whine with fright. In morning light, sure enough, there were the Monster's tracks. Plainly, Ragnar saw where the Wolverine sneaked up-wind on the dogs. A hollow in the snow revealed where he'd crouched for hours, watching the dogs, waiting for the Man-Thing. Ragnar knew that the Old Wolverine was filled with hatred and resentment. Even now he was likely planning his next foul deed.

To Ragnar, the wolverine had, over time, gained a personality as surely as Moby Dick had infiltrated Captain Ahab's mind. Ragnar had a name for him: he called him 'Ol' Sunvabich.' This night in Trappers Hall, as we listened to the tale, we ourselves came to detest the Beast. We hoped he would get it in the end. It would serve him right for all the damage he'd done and all the killing and the fouling.

However, I held a secret feeling that the Old Fellow was in his right place, and that Ragnar was the Intruder. After all, Ol' Sunvabich's ancestors owned these northern forests. For eons they had ruled this domain. Now a Creature stalked him and meant to kill him. Why?

My thoughts had wandered for a moment but Ragnar's voice pulled me back. He was in full flight. He held the floor. His audience was spellbound. As I listened, I heard a bitter and vengeful hatred rise up in Ragnar's tone as he recounted the Wolverine's vile acts. How the man loathed the animal! How he hated its foul odor and the brute's mean and despicable ways. Ragnar even hated the sight of Ol' Sunvabich. He despised the animal's shape, with its high rear-end and belly low to the ground. He hated, too, the slouching humped-over gait. He found the sharply pointed head and face abhorrent.

Ragnar finally had had enough of the Wolverine's depredations. He vowed he would track down and kill Ol' Sunvabich if it was the last thing he ever did. There was not enough space in the North Country for the two of them. Ragnar intended to win. He would start as soon as the first snow had covered the land. And once on the animal's track, he'd follow and follow and run him to earth, and put a slug in that fiendish skull.

Ol' Sunvabich

The decision meant that Ragnar would forego serious trapping for as long as it took to hunt down the Evil One—the entire winter if necessary. About mid-November he set out, traveling light. He packed a light sled and took three dogs. On the sled he carried a minimum of camping gear, a high-powered rifle, ammunition, Pemmican, and a small supply of food for the dogs. Mostly though, he would live off the country.

In deep snow and frigid weather, Ragnar circled his trapline. He was positive that he would meet up with the wolverine somewhere around its perimeter. It took four days of hard slogging to complete the ninety-nine mile circuit. In those four days Ragnar saw not one sign—not one footprint—of his archenemy.

Near the beginning of the second lap around the trapline, however, Ragnar met the well-known track but noted that it was a few days old. A study of signs showed for the full circuit.

Outwitted again! Ragnar was furious. He swore bitter vengeance against his foe. The wolverine had maintained a distance of a half-mile or so behind the man and dogteam. The signs revealed that every night he would burrow down in the snow within sight of Ragnar's tent. Never once, however, did he show his presence by resorting to any of his mischievous and Satanic tricks. He followed, and watched and waited—and possibly, he planned.

The hunt was a long, hard and grueling ordeal. Every day Ragnar tracked and searched for the telltale footprints. Storms and wind would often obliterate a fresh trail, and it might be some hours or days before he would locate the track again. Twice, they came upon one another unexpectedly. With such relentless pressure the Wolverine's natural hatred for his pursuer developed to even more sinister proportions. His normally mean behavioral characteristics, now tormented by Ragnar's daily persistence, drove him to bolder actions. Ol' Sunvabich resorted to heinous treachery.

He caught and maimed Ragnar's lead dog. He fouled the last supply of Pemmican. On one cold, dark night he ripped a wide gash in the tent. The long, sharp claws—that were capable of disemboweling a full-grown bear—missed Ragnar's head only by inches.

Ragnar drove himself and his ailing dogs to longer and longer days. They were living on reduced rations. Food supplies were low—all because of the stealthy, plundering, despoiling ways of the brute. Ragnar would often sit up late into the night and keep watch, his rifle cocked and in his hands. The dogs retired nearby—curled up asleep in the snow. The long vigil might continue for hours. Eventually he would fall asleep from sheer fatigue. It was then that the Old Hellion would sneak in close and leave his hateful mark.

In bitter winter weather the two enemies trailed and hunted each other. Their paths crossed occasionally. There were a few sudden, unexpected close encounters. Somehow the wolverine eluded a confrontation. Ragnar now saw him every day. On two occasions the Beast was close enough that Ragnar raised his rifle. As usual, however, the wolverine was just out of range of the deadly weapon. Once, Ragnar raised the long gun-barrel and brought the 'Carcajou' into his sights! In that same instant the target vanished into thin air.

The chase continued—grim and unrelenting.

One night the scene changed: a fresh snowfall laid down a two-foot depth of white powder. In the morning light the animal's tracks were clear and fresh—and close by the camp!

Ragnar took only the time needed to tie on his snowshoes. He grabbed his rifle and a handful of shells. He was away on a steady shuffling run along the wolverine's hot track. The dogs were left at camp, tied to their stakes. Ragnar was dressed lightly, and he set himself a rapid pace. The temperature was well below zero, but with the exertion required to plow through the deep snow, Ragnar warmed to his task.

The Wolverine soon came into view about 400 yards away, heaving mightily in long jumps through the soft snow. The powdery layer hampered his movements. At each jump he was partly concealed until he thrust himself forward once more. In a half-hour chase Ragnar gained steadily on the laboring animal. With an all-out effort, he closed the distance to about 300 yards.

He swung the rifle to his shoulder and, in that same split second, fired a shot. This was the first he had made in the pursuit! Never had Ol' Sunvabich been so clear in his sights. Never had the animal been within rifle range. Ragnar was alive with anticipation as he watched for the animal to fall and lie still.

In telling, Ragnar digressed for a while to convince us that he was a crack shot. He bragged of the game he has brought down from 'nearly a quarter-mile away.' He told yarns about his hunting prowess and his ability with a rifle.

"It's been years," he said, "since I wasted even one bullet!" Our group was silent, withholding our verdict. Ragnar refreshed himself with a long drink of beer and continued with his story.

Ragnar watched. In amazement, he saw that the animal still plunged through the soft snow!

Ol' Sunvabich was making tracks in that awkward humped-over gait. Ragnar was sure he had hit him. He had aimed dead center at the animal's posterior. There was no way he could have missed that broad target—especially as close as 300 yards.

Ragnar raced to the spot where he had shot at his quarry. He looked first for signs of blood in the white snow—even a few drops would be significant. There was no trail of blood, no change in the spacing of his leaps. The imprints of the tracks leading away were identical with earlier signs.

Ragnar kept up the pace and the pressure. Seldom now was Ol' Sunvabich out of his sight. The distance between the two held constant for the next mile or so. The wolverine stayed just out of rifle range—as if he knew exactly the effective reach of the weapon Ragnar carried.

It was early afternoon. Ragnar had covered ten or fifteen miles on snowshoes in soft snow. Part of the trek had led him through spruce forests and along the edge of the lakes. He was feeling the strain. His legs were weary. The cold was seeping into his bones. He felt low in energy. Reaching into his small pack he found the last piece of Pemmican that the wolverine had not fouled. This he chewed on as he took up the chase again.

The country had suddenly become more rolling. Every climb drained energy from man and beast. Both were slowing. The Hunted One held a set interval from the Hunter.

On a steep upgrade, barren of trees, the gap between the two enemies narrowed. The Wolverine began a long, steep climb, while Ragnar was on a downhill trot toward the base of the small valley. The space between them closed a few more critical yards. Ragnar saw his chance. This time he took careful aim—moving the rifle barrel in unison with his target's rhythmic undulations. "I'll hit him in the rear-end when the tail is raised," Ragnar told himself. "That'll send the bullet through the hole in the loathsome body. It'll lodge in his mean little brain."

Before he squeezed the trigger, Ragnar, filled with frustration and hate, spoke aloud of his old Enemy. "That way, there'll be no other hole in the fur when I hang your stinkin' hide on the outside of my cabin wall!"

Ragnar fired. A shout of exultation burst from him as the bullet sped on its way. For the second time that day the hunter watched for the Wolverine to tumble in the snow—to move no more. For the second time that day, the animal did not slacken pace! Again there was no change in his ungainly leaps though the heavy snow.

Stunned and unbelieving, Ragnar stood at the spot where the Wolverine should have now been lying lifeless. It had been years since he had to fire twice at any game. The first shot had always met its mark. In frantic desperation, again at a half-run, Ragnar checked his rifle. He looked hard at his few remaining bullets. Was he losing his sight? Dreaming? He felt positive that his shot had been a bull's-eye—right on target.

Now, Ragnar sensed that something had changed: the old wolverine had slowed a bit. His leaps were shorter. The fresh tracks revealed two places where he had sunk down flat on the snow. He had rested for a few seconds at each place.

Ragnar redoubled his effort. His half-run was demanding of his fast-reducing store of energy. He emptied his pockets of every non-essential and threw off his pack. He had to run his enemy to earth now. He had to finish him off before the light began to fade.

"Now...,...," Ragnar kept repeating the word in a sort of delirium. "It has to be NOW!"

Ragnar increased his speed. He was on a full-out run—in full extension of all his physical powers. His lungs worked like a blacksmith's bellows. Loud, hoarse wheezes choked from his throat with every forward lunge.

Only a hundred yards ahead, Ol' Sunvabich exploded out of a steep-sided snowdrift, sending showers of the white-stuff flying around him. Thrusts of his broad feet propelled him forward like a toboggan on a downhill run.

The Wolverine now ran for its life on a flat, snow-packed stretch of ground. Ragnar waited a few seconds to quiet his heaving lungs. Again he synchronized the rhythm of the rifle with the surging body. For the third time, when the tail was raised, Ragnar fired a shot at his fleeing target. This time he knew it had found its mark. It had felt right. It had sounded right.

The wolverine dropped in its tracks. Like a stone he dropped. The body lay spread-out and unmoving on the snow, Ragnar felt him. There was no heartbeat.

Ol' Sunvabich was dead.

He had sprawled as he died. His four feet widespread as if he was still running. His head, flat on the snow, pointed in the direction he had been heading. The tail lay straight behind him. There was not a drop of blood on the snow. Ragnar could not find a bullet hole or wound of any kind on the body.

Ragnar was mystified. He was at a loss to explain these unreal, almost eerie, happenings. He continued to examine the dead animal. He scrutinized every part of the body. Finally he opened the mouth and peered inside.

There, on the flat, slightly curled-up tongue lay three lead slugs!

Ragnar crouched where he was—shocked into immobility. It was biting cold but the man did not move for many minutes. He pondered this remarkable and uncanny discovery. Again he studied the creature's mouth. In minute detail he re-examined the lips, the roof of the mouth and each tooth. The only evidence he could find of anything out of the ordinary, were faint lead-like markings on the backside of the large canine teeth. ***He found two telltale marks on the upper right tooth—and only one such mark on the upper left tooth!***

Ragnar recovered the three slugs from the wolverine's tongue and placed them inside an inner pocket of his jacket. He tied a short cord around the animal's tail and slung Ol' Sunvabich over his shoulder. There the Beast hung; head down, swaying from side to side with each weary step that Ragnar made on the long trek back to camp. During every pace of the twenty miles of plodding, Ragnar cudgeled his brain over each action and each minor detail of the event. He knew he had fired three times at Ol' Sunvabich. He knew that each shot had been timed to strike when the tail was raised. Finally Ragnar concluded that at each shot—as planned—he had sent a bullet into the animal's posterior!

It had been a long story. As we sat around Trappers Hall Ragnar had held us enthralled. He had acted out all parts of the drama. Now for a half-minute, all was silent. Ragnar didn't move. He let the story sink in and penetrate our very bones. The silence held. Not a man broke the spell. We sensed there was more to come.

In the yellow gloom of the coal-oil lamp, Ragnar eventually moved. He reached into an inside pocket of his jacket and then held his hand toward the light for all to see. There—there, on his large, callused palm lay three slightly flattened lead slugs.

We gazed at these 'artifacts.' I visualized each one traveling through the body of Ol' Sunvabich and striking a longtooth. Then—spent of energy—each slug fell onto the slight hollow of the Wolverine's tongue.

As Ragnar prepared to leave Trappers Hall for his canoe trip across the Fon du Lac, we looked again at the bullet slugs. Most of us marveled and wondered and questioned—and some were skeptical. I, however, preferred to Believe. Strange things happen, so it is said, in this land of the Midnight Sun.

On his way out, Ragnar's voice continued to fill the Hall: "Yeah," he was saying, "those slugs are the proof. Come to my place tomorrow and I'll show you the hide. Not a hole in it— except one. Yeah—I finally got Ol' Sunvabich in the end!"

NOTE: *This story is nearly identical to the one Ragnar related to Debbie and me. The major difference was where Ragnar opened the mouth of the old devil wolverine and peered inside. "There on the flat, slightly curled up tongue," he said, "I found a slug" (Actually he fired only one shot. Not three, as he had told the group in Stony Rapids).*

6

Jonsson Island

The whiskey jacks had disappeared into the bush while we listened to Ragnar's story. Now they were bothering us again. One noisy jay fluttered in and landed on Ragnar's cap. Debbie picked up her camera but wasn't quick enough to shoot a picture before the bird flew off. Then, lifting the cover of the Dry Box, she pulled out packages of Cracker Jack for each of us saying, "It's time for a snack. Now you can feed your pets, Mr. Jonnson."

"Thanks!" Ragnar replied, then continued. "I have some lumps of sugar in my pocket. Could we have a cup of tea?"

"Good idea." Debbie dipped a pot of water from the lake while I set up the Coleman stove and the tea was soon ready. As we munched, I asked Ragnar if he ever knew Eskimo Charlie, whom I had read about in ***Sleeping Island*** by Prentice Downes, and also in the recent spring issue of *The Beaver* by Robert H. Cockburn.

"Eskimo Charlie! Oh! Sure! Yeah! I knew him. He lived over on Putahow Lake. His real name was Charlie Planinshek. He was Yugoslavian. There's also a lake they call Charlie. Yeah! I knew him well," he chuckled. "He was a character! He was a big talker. He talked loud, he talked dirty and he talked a lot. He had no use for the Chips and they knew it. The Chips around here are good people and they certainly did put up with a lot from Charlie. He claimed the whole area around Putahow, Goose and Charlie Lake as his own property. He told the Chips to stay away. Whenever he found a trap set by one of them, he would make off with the trap as well as anything caught in their traps.

"He was a gardener. He grew lettuce, radishes, onions, cabbage and the like and he would hang up human skulls each mounted on a pole to keep the Chips away. Before I first met him, Charlie had gone by canoe all the way to Sonora in Mexico. He had some relatives down there. He was gone for a few years. He told me, he came back around the Gulf of Mexico, Florida and up the East Coast, also by canoe, to Montreal and all the way back up here.

"He had fixed up an old wagon, which he used for hauling in poles to be cut for firewood, animals he shot and the like. His dog team was trained to pull his wagon. He told me that once he raised a young moose whose mother he had shot. And he trained that moose to team up with his dogs when they hauled the wagon.

"Charlie died a long time ago. Must have been early in 1944. I hadn't seen or heard anything of him for several months. Then my old friend Constable Marcel Chappius of the R.C.M.P. came along on his winter patrol in 1945, I guess it was. He told me he had just found the remains of Eskimo Charlie in his cabin and thought he must have been dead for more than a year."

"Do you know about the starving Eskimos that the government flew down to this lake in 1950?" Ragnar asked.

"I've read about it somewhere," I replied.

"That was a bad deal! They flew down forty-nine Eskimos in the spring and put them on Jonsson Island. They were going to make commercial fishermen of them. They were to work for Chuipka and Canadian Fisheries. Those Eskimos you know had been starving over along the Kazan below Ennadai and the small lakes to the east. The Windy River Post closed down in 1948, you see, and there was no longer a place for them to trade. They were out of shells for their rifles and the deer even failed to pass through the hills where the hunters watched day after day. Many of those people died from the lack of food even though they did catch fish until their nets were worn out. So Ottawa decided to round up the survivors and they flew them right down here. Yeah! They brought forty-nine of them right down to Nueltin and put them on Jonsson Island."

"Jonsson Island," I cut in. "How far is that from here?"

"About twenty miles over to the northeast," he replied, swinging his arm in that direction. "I was at my camp over in Hearne Bay that spring. When I came back to my island in July, it was quite a surprise to find all those people on Jonsson Island. That's my island, you see. It has been my base, the place I've called home ever since I came up here in 1939. Those people over-ran the island but they did stay away from my cabin, teepee and equipment. The Fisheries men did eventually move them across the channel to Todd Island. That's a bigger island you see."

"Could you speak their language?"

"No. Only a few words. I had met a few of them in earlier years at Windy River Post. One of them had learned to speak both English and Chip, so with his help, we could communicate with the others pretty well. He was the shaman of the group. A good man."

"What was his name?"

"Pamala," Ragnar replied.

"Oh yes! I've read about him. I think it was in the book by Francis Harper titled ***Caribou Eskimos of the Upper Kazan***."

"That's right. I read that one, too. Pamala was a very good man, as were they all. The Chuipka men tried to teach them to use motor boats to lift the nets and that sort of thing but those Eskimos just didn't comprehend or like working for money. When the 1950 season ended, right after freeze up, the entire group walked back to their home country down river from Ennadai Lake. Several more of them starved to death that winter. They had no place to trade, as Windy River Post had closed two years before. I was so sorry for those people but there was no way I could help much." Ragnar sat quietly shaking his head. "I still feel sad, there was nothing I could do to help."

"It was a year or two later, as I recall, the few who did manage to survive were again picked up and this time flown to Rankin Inlet. Is that right, Ragnar?"

"Yes. I think it was in 1956. Charles Schweder deserves a lot of credit for keeping some of them alive. He did all he could to get food and supplies flown in to them even after the Windy River Post was closed. The government eventually built houses for them and the men found work in the nickel mines."

"We used to fly in with Chuipka Airways when we came north in the early years. Were those the same people who did the commercial fishing around here?" I asked.

"The very same. Chuipka came in here and he had a camp over on Big Sand Beach. He brought his equipment up in the fall and unloaded it only one foot above the water and in 1960 high water came and washed it all out into the lake," Ragnar laughed. "Hundreds of gallons of gas and all the equipment. They never found it again. They fished Nueltin for several years. There used to be seals in the north part of this lake. Chuipka's crew shot all of those animals, you see, because the seals used to get tangled in their nets. Now there are no more seals in either Nueltin or Seal Hole Lakes. Chuipka is now retired. He lives south of Dolphin, Manitoba. That's where he is. He never made any money with his fishing."

"My son and a couple of his cousins were in Brochet with me back in 1964.

The HBC manager showed us several boxes of mail waiting for you there. He was expecting you to come and pick it up that summer. It had been five years since he had seen you and he said you regularly came down every fourth or fifth year to trade and pick up your mail. Did you make it to Brochet that year?"

"No. My last canoe trip to Brochet was in 1957 with a young lad from here. A good kid named Ovide Denecheze. He was sixteen at the time. Now he's one of the guides at Tree Line Lodge. Tom Lamb must have brought those boxes of mail to me. He had been flying out my furs and bringing in supplies from Churchill for a few years. I flew to Churchill with Tom in 1961. Then he died. Guess it was about 1963. In later years Hank Parsons, Bob Ferguson and Bob Burgess took care of those things for me."

"The HBC manager also told us that while you were in Brochet in 1946, people were still talking about the war and you asked why there was so much discussion about the war as it had been twenty-eight years since the war had ended. You were told there had been another war, World War II, and this was news to you as you had been out of contact with civilization since you had last been down to pick up your mail in 1941. Is that story true?" I asked.

He sat there with a big grin on his face. "Not exactly," he laughed, slapping his knee. "No. I was just having a little fun with 'em down there."

The west wind began to pick up so we decided to head back toward our tents and Tree Line Lodge at mid-day. Paddling along Ragnar remarked, "I really like this canoe. I'd like to buy it. How much do you want for it?"

"Sorry to say, we can't sell it. This one was loaned to us by some friends."

Following breakfast the next morning, we returned to the Lodge under sunny skies to visit again with Ragnar. We found him in a jovial mood. He had received some good news the previous afternoon. He would be flying outside again on July 23. "I'm going to the hospital in Winnipeg to have a cataract removed from my left eye. 'Guess you know I went down there more'n a year ago and had my shootin' eye fixed."

"Yes. We read about it in our local daily newspaper. You'll get another look at some of those pretty nurses."

"Yeah," he grinned. "I look forward to that. When I come back I'll even be able to read the fine print. It'll be good to have another look at the big city but I hope I don't have to stay down there very long. I'll need to clean myself up as best I can. Those nurses can be mighty fussy. It's hard to keep neat'n clean out here in the bush."

He proceeded to tell us a story he thought to be extremely funny. The story was written up in the book ***Sleeping Island***. Ragnar kept chuckling, as he retold the story, which he said was originally told to Prentiss G. Downes in 1939 by a man named Charlie who used to live at Reindeer Lake.

"One day in the winter," Charlie said to Downes, "I was going along the big part of the lake where there are no islands. It was all just white and flat as far as you could see. I needed meat for myself and the dogs. Stopping and looking over the snow, I saw two little black things away out on the lake. They were walking back and forth very slowly. I fired my rifle at them, and then I fired again. I did not hit either of them, for they kept right on walking back and forth, quite undisturbed. I could not understand why my shooting was so poor. Then I fired twice more. By golly! You know when I put my gun down and wiped my eyes, I found that those two caribou were a couple of lice walking back and forth on my eyebrows!"

Ragnar concluded the story, still laughing, by saying "That old man who used to live at Reindeer Lake was none other than Eskimo Charlie."

When the laughter subsided, I spoke up. "Back in 1964 we were at Reindeer Lake Lodge. The old fellow who owned the place told us that before coming to Reindeer, he had run a trap line at Nueltin Lake for more than twenty years. Did you ever know a John Ivanchuk?"

"Yes. I knew him quite well. He was a partner of Eskimo Charlie's."

Wanting to know more about some of the other old timers and history of the area, I asked about I. H. 'Windy' Smith. Ragnar told us that Windy Smith was one of the early free-traders with posts for a while near Smith Bay and another up the Thlewiaza along the Old North Trail at Smith-House Lake. Ragnar went on to say, "He was also a trapper and prospector. 'Guess he did quite well. He went back outside while still a fairly young man."

"Did you know Joe Highway?"

"Yes. Sure! He was a good friend of mine. In fact, one of my best friends. I first met him one summer at Nueltin Lake Post back in the '40s. Joe was one of the freighters who paddled and portaged freight back and forth for the HBC out of Brochet. He liked it up here and north in the barrens. Joe worked for a few years at Nueltin Lake Post with Fred Schweder before he went to trapping on his own. While at the post he learned from the Eskimos, who came in to trade, the best ways to catch white foxes. He even learned how to speak their language. Then he went to trapping up toward Hicks Lake. Joe did quite well out there. One year he brought in more than 300 fox skins. He even tried to talk me into going north with him but I decided to stay down this way. It's cold enough for me near Nueltin in the wintertime. I like it better where there are some trees to help break the wind. Joe had several kids. When he and his wife decided their children should have some schooling, he built them a house in Brochet. They moved away. But he still came back to trap for a few more years and he also worked here at Tree Line Lodge as a guide when it was first built. I haven't seen him for the past three or four years."

"Ragnar, can you tell us a little about the Schweders at Nueltin Lake Post?"

"Well, let's see now. When I first came up this way, Fred Schweder had started to trade at the mouth of the Windy River. Before that he had been the factor at the Hudson's Bay Post up near the junction of the Red and Windy Rivers. He built a nice setup near the mouth of Windy River. He and his family were there for a couple of years. Then Fred, Sr. gave it up in 1946, I think it was. He went to fishing at Reindeer Lake and his children went to school in The Pas.

"When they moved away, the oldest son, Charles, continued to operate the post for a couple of more years with the help of his brother, Fred, Jr. I used to get in to the Windy Post every few months. You see, I have a teepee east of Windy Lake. Their place made a handy spot for me, when I needed some supplies. But the Schweder boys gave it up and went to Churchill in 1948, so I lost my nearby place to trade."

My mind flashed back to the book ***People of the Deer*** by Farley Mowat. My suspicions were that the author of the book had written about the Schweder family and had most likely given them assumed names. So I asked Ragnar if he had read the Farley Mowat book.

"Sure did," he grinned. "Around here we call Farley Mowat 'Hardly Knowit,'" Ragnar laughed and continued. "Mowat had a hard time recording his facts correctly. He was at Windy River in 1947 all right, so the boys told me. I didn't get to see him. His story was indeed built around the Schweder family and the things he had learned from Charles and Fredie."

"Were there any girls in the Schweder family?"

"Yes. There were four girls and also younger sons named Mike and Norman. And there was a little boy. 'Can't think of his name right now."

"Yesterday we talked about Francis Harper who spent several months with the boys in 1947 and, as you know, his book contains information about the Eskimos who used to visit Windy River Post. It also tells about the two starving Eskimo children rescued by Charles Schweder. Do you recall seeing them there?"

"Sure. Cute youngsters. Very intelligent, too. Charles adopted them and when he and Fredie went to Churchill, those children went along. Let's see now—Anoteelik was the boy's name and his sister was Rita. They must be all grown up, with families of their own by now."

"Ragnar, you've lived in Canada for sixty years. Did you ever get back to Sweden to visit your family?"

"No." He paused. "Used to correspond with 'em once in a while when I was young. But guess there's none of 'em alive any more. Except one. I have a nephew. He lives in B.C."

My questions had been answered. Debbie and I still had three days before our pick up date. I asked Ragnar where he would suggest we go to catch a fish and find good camping places.

"The lake trout are in deep water this time of year. You might get a jackfish near the mouth of the river," he replied. "For camping there are great places along a sand ridge over to the northeast, about ten or twelve miles from here."

It was a picture perfect day. Earlier Ragnar had asked how he could get a copy of ***Cold Summer Wind,*** which had recently been published. I promised to send him a copy when we returned to Michigan. Right after lunch we took photos, said our good-byes and paddled away. We fished the mouth of the Thlewiaza and also found the esker Ragnar told us about. Such a beautiful place but we failed to catch a single fish.

Ragnar Jonsson was one of a kind, certainly a very special person. He was the last of the great, white trappers. There will never be another like him. Some day we will return to Nueltin Lake, and spend some time on Jonsson Island where I know we will feel his presence in that remote and wonderful land.

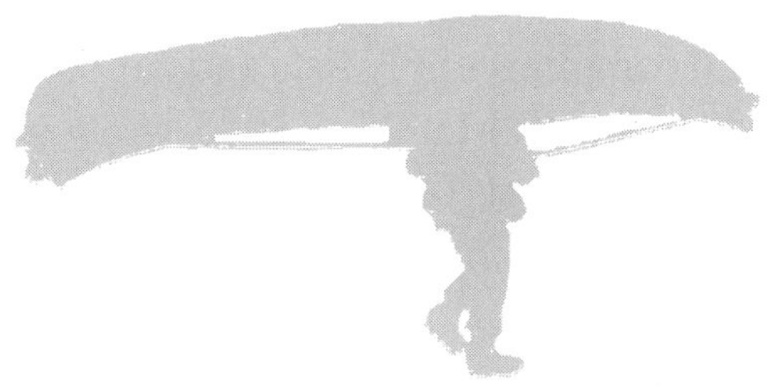

7

Colville Lake

Seven years frittered away since Darrell and I had paddled together in northern Canada. In those years, Darrell had advanced to become the President and General Manager of the family fertilizer business. It was August when he said, "Dad, how would you like to go canoeing with me next summer?"

"That would be great," I replied. "Where would we go?"

"It doesn't make a lot of difference to me, as long as it's somewhere in Northern Canada. Where would you like to go?"

"Oh boy!" I replied. Then cautiously added, "What I'd really like to do is canoe the Anderson River. We could start at Colville Lake. That way we could spend some time with Bern Will Brown. We would be above the Arctic Circle and we could canoe right on down to the Arctic Ocean."

I had corresponded with Bern several times by dog-sled mail since he first read ***Cold Summer Wind***, shortly after it was published in the fall of 1983. So we already knew a little about each other, but found there was much more to learn.

I really expected Darrell to say that he couldn't be away from the business for such a long time, but without hesitation he responded, "Sounds good to me. Let's plan on it."

"Excellent!" I was overjoyed at the thought! "Maybe we'll finally get to cross the Arctic Circle and actually see the midnight sun." This was being consistent with the past. Each time the two of us had traveled together during our quarter of a century of canoeing, we had gone farther to the northwest.

Plans continued to develop during the autumn. We ordered maps and discussed the possibility of buying a new, lightweight canoe of modern design. "It would be nice if Debbie could go with us," Darrell remarked during one of our chats in December. "What would you think if I ask her?"

"I'd like it. But I don't know if she could get away from work."

"Maybe she could get a leave of absence."

Debbie's answer was "yes." She would like to go. Then it was full speed ahead with the planning. We prepared food and camping supply lists and, among other things, corresponded with Bern Will Brown. By March of 1985 we had decided to drive our pickup truck to Inuvik, Northwest Territories. There we would engage a bush pilot to fly us, along with our camping equipment, the final 220 miles to Colville Lake.

We were uncertain just how we would return from the mouth of the Anderson River to Inuvik, but we prepared to paddle out across Liverpool Bay and cross the peninsula to the Inuit settlement of Tuktoyaktyuk. Then, if time permitted, we would move into the Mackenzie River delta and upstream to Inuvik.

A new Mad River Monarch Canoe arrived during the final week of May. We are fortunate to have as a friend the number one canoeist in North America, Verlen Kruger. He is also the designer of the Monarch, one of which he used on his 28,000-mile Ultimate Canoe Challenge. In early June, we took the Monarch to Verlen's home on the banks of the Grand River in Lansing, Michigan. He had offered to help us outfit it for wilderness travel. He showed us how to install the spray cover and adjust the seat. He installed several additional layers of Kevlar cloth to the inside of the deck, strengthening it considerably, and put in several extra shock chord loops.

"I sure would like to be going with you," Verlen said while working away. "I have a complete set of maps for that trip. At one time I had planned to cross Great Bear Lake and portage over into the headwaters of the Anderson and then on down to the Polar Sea."

Verlen would accept no pay for those several hours of work. As we drove away, after thanking him, we were gratefully aware that our Monarch had certainly received 'the master's touch.'

Excitement and anticipation began to build during those final weeks prior to departure. In addition to our usual work, there were the final plans including shopping and packing food for each day of the journey. The food detail was handled by Darrell as he had agreed to be our chief cook, "providing Dad will prepare the breakfasts and Deb will do the dishes."

There was physical training for each of us. Debbie jogged six miles or more each day, Darrell rode his bike from twelve to thirty miles a day and I continued my usual daily walking and jogging of three to seven miles.

Three times per week we took the canoes to either the Shiawassee River or the Lobdell Lakes for workouts of up to seven hours of steady paddling. We each trained for portaging the canoes and packs.

We were underway at 3:30 on the morning of Friday, July 5, 1985. It was west and north for the next four days. The following Monday afternoon we completed the 4,000-mile drive up the Alaska Highway to Whitehorse, Yukon Territory. Securing a room at Regina Inn overlooking the Yukon River, I delivered a case of books to Maxmillian's Gold Rush Emporium which they had ordered from Wilderness Adventure Books about ten days earlier.

The following morning we were off to drive to Dawson City. Along the way and throughout the Yukon, the roadsides were ablaze with fireweed, the official flower of the Yukon Territory. Interesting stops were made at Lake Laberge, Five Fingers Rapids and Pelly Crossing before arrival in old Dawson City.

By the time we had checked into the Eldorado Hotel and had supper that rainy evening, we were too late to catch the show at either the Palace Grand or Diamond Tooth Gertie's. I was in time, however, to deliver several copies of ***One Incredible Journey*** to the bookstore and meet its interesting and colorful manager, one Lowry Toombs.

Before calling it a day, we walked the muddy streets to visit the cabin of poet Robert W. Service, but were a little late to see him, as he died in Lancieux, France back in 1958. But, it was certainly a pleasure to view the place from

Five Fingers Rapids—Yukon River

where he had written those great poems of Canada's North Country and the gold rush.

Wednesday was a most memorable day. It was raining as we drove the twenty-three miles back alongside the Klondike River to the south end of the Dempster Highway. Moving north through the Ogilvie Mountains, we soon broke out into the sunshine. Construction crews were working to improve some of the early built sections of the highway, which was first opened in 1979. The Eagle Plains Hotel, with its fine restaurant and service station, was the only business along the entire 360 miles of the Dempster south of Fort McPherson. Needless to say, everyone traveling the highway stops there. It provided us an enjoyable break.

While having lunch in the dining room we struck up a conversation with a man at an adjoining table. He was an old time Yukoner who spoke on several topics in the few minutes we were exposed to his line of palaver. The most memorable item we carried away was his statement that sunflowers cannot be grown above the Arctic Circle. The reason he gave was that sunflowers always keep their faces toward the sun. When the sun remains above the horizon during all twenty-four hours for day after day, the plants keep turning until they twist their heads off.

It was shortly after 2:00 when we arrived at the Arctic Circle, thirty-five

The author arrives at the Arctic Circle

miles north of Eagle Plains. This was the first time any of us had been so far north. In 1978 Darrell and I had been within forty-six miles of the 'circle,' while paddling down the Back River. It had taken me more than sixty years to get to the Arctic Circle and I was overjoyed to be there. Jogging back and forth, in an elongated circle, within three minutes, I had crossed the Arctic Circle nine times.

Then a couple of hours later an almost unbelievable thing happened. A new set of steel-belted radials had been installed on our vehicle in Michigan prior to departure. Stopping on a hilltop in the Richardson Mountains to stretch our legs, we were shocked by what we observed. Neither rear tire was flat but both were rapidly leaking air. "Can you believe that!?" Darrell sputtered as he pulled out the jack. "Nearly four thousand miles without any trouble and now we have two flats at the same time."

"And, if we hadn't stopped right here," Deb replied, "both of those new tires would probably have been ruined." Fortunately, we were carrying two spares.

Soon we crossed the summit and entered Northwest Territories. Then came the Peel and Mackenzie River crossings on the free ferries and, by nine in the evening, we rolled into Inuvik. Finding a room in that bustling town was something else. All four hotels were solidly booked. Following supper and on the way to the campground to set up our tents, we checked again at the Finto Motor Inn. Fortunately, they had received a cancellation.

As midnight approached, Deb and I drove around for a better look at the settlement while Darrell walked up on a hill to watch and photograph the midnight sun. Inuvik is a unique settlement. It was built by the Canadian government in the late 1950s and early '60s. It was designed to serve as the main center for administration, communications, education and medical care for Canada's Western Arctic. It is also used as the terminus for mineral, oil and gas exploration and development in the Mackenzie River delta, the Beaufort Sea and the Arctic Islands.

The name Inuvik is the Inuit word for 'Place of Man.' It is a modern town and, because of the permafrost, the utilities, including water and heat, are piped through heated utilidors above the surface of the ground. Inuvik is situated on high ground along the east shore of the East Channel of the Mackenzie Delta. It was accessible only by river or air until the 460-mile Dempster Highway was opened. Inuvik is the home of more than three thousand people, making it the largest settlement above the Arctic Circle in North America.

The Aklak Air people were expecting us. With two Cessna 185s and a canoe bound tightly above the right pontoon of each, we were soon underway to the Hareskin Indian settlement of Colville Lake. It was a good flight and, as we taxied up to the dock, Bern Will Brown stood waiting for us. As I popped the Cessna 185's door open, he said, "You must be Clate."

"That's right, and you are Bern."

"Welcome to Colville Lake Lodge! It's so nice to meet you."

"It certainly is a pleasure," Debbie and Darrell were introduced to Bern. Unloading the canoes and gear, we made our way up to the Lodge where we met Margaret Brown.

Bern grew up near Rochester, New York. He always loved the north and, because of the challenge he saw, became a Roman Catholic missionary in 1948. Then, for the next twenty-two years, he served both Indians and Eskimos at various widespread settlements across Canada's northern territories. In 1962, Father Brown was sent to Colville Lake to establish a mission for the Hareskin Indians, who are known by the neighboring tribes as 'The End of the Earth People.' Bern traveled to Colville by canoe with a few supplies and seven sled dogs. Upon arrival, he found about twenty-five Indians living nearby, so he pitched his tent and soon began erecting a mission building from the black spruce trees, which grow around the lake. For the next several years, with the help of the local Indians, he helped build log homes for each family residing in the settlement. His first duty, which he diligently pursued, was to the Indians and to his church.

In 1971, the Vatican issued a dispensation from celibacy to Father Brown, so that he could marry Margaret. This remarkable Eskimo girl was one of fourteen children and grew up on the Arctic coast east of Paulatuk. Her father was born in Texas and spent his life as a trapper while her mother is of Eskimo stock. As a teenager she was sent to Inuvik to attend school. The Bishop flew in to marry Bern and Margaret in the delightful log church, known as 'Our Lady of the Snows' mission, where Bern still carries on as pastor. The beautiful, large mural at the front of the sanctuary depicting 'Our Lady of the Snows' was done by artist Bern.

"There are six girls canoeing your route," said Bern. "They left here yesterday and you'll probably overtake them within a day or two."

"Is that right!" I replied with surprise. "We expected to be the only ones to do the Anderson this year."

"They're all eighteen-year-olds except one. Some of them are still in school. I hope you will stay with them, at least until they get through Falcon Canyon. I'm worried that unless you do, they may not make it. They looked so inexperienced."

I added, "They'll probably make it all right but we'll keep an eye out for them."

Following lunch, Bern showed us around the settlement. There was a store serving the area, known as Kapami Co-op Ltd. We visited the conference building and the fine museum containing both Indian and Inuit artifacts, many of

Clayton Klein visits with Bern Will Brown

which we had not seen anywhere before. Above the museum, Bern took us into his well-lighted studio where we enjoyed looking at some of his wonderful oil paintings, of which he was producing forty-five to fifty each year. His paintings are in great demand as he is considered to be one of Canada's foremost northern artists. Just as Remington painted the historical West in America in the nineteenth century, today Bern Will Brown is painting historical scenes of Canada's northern frontier. He is putting on canvas the beautiful homeland of the Inuit and Indian and capturing their old way of life that is so rapidly disappearing. His paintings hang today in museum and government offices in Yellowknife and Ottawa and in many private collections across both the United States and Canada.

As the conversation continued to flow, we walked over to look at some of Margaret's dogs. She and Bern have developed a breed of fine, white malamutes, one of which was about to give birth to a litter of puppies. Each malamute had its own house, also constructed of logs. We then went into the underground refrigerator room where the temperature remains at 22° Fahrenheit the year around. To construct it, Bern had dug into the hillside permafrost to a depth of thirty-five feet. Several quarters of caribou and piles of frozen trout and whitefish were being stored inside. All of the buildings in the settlement, including the Lodge's outhouse, were constructed from the black spruce trees around the lake. "We just finished varnishing everything last week," he said. "We clean and varnish all of the buildings, inside and out, each spring."

Margaret prepared a wonderful dinner for us consisting of several of her specialties, including a caribou roast. Everything was delicious. Then, as the visiting continued, Bern brought out a guest autograph book for us to sign. Handing it to Darrell, he said, "I'd like to have you and Debbie sign in this one. Clate, I'd like you to sign in another book." He soon brought out his 'Special Guest' autograph book and handed it to me, saying, "This is the one I'd like you to autograph."

Glancing at it and seeing who some of his earlier guests had been, I said, "I don't think I rate this one. Are you certain you want my signature in here?"

"I definitely do," he replied. "You are our special guest today, just as those others were in the past."

So, I added my signature below some prominent people, such as Prince Charles of England, former Canadian Prime Minister Pierre Trudeau and Commissioner Stuart M. Hodgson of Northwest Territories.

Later we went over our maps of the Ross and Anderson Rivers. Bern and Margaret took twenty-seven days in 1976 to canoe those 410 miles. He marked on the maps certain things we should watch for such as the rapids, waterfalls, canyon, old buildings, the location of the old Hudson's Bay Company's Fort Anderson and a hillside made up of sea fossils.

Just before 9:00 that evening, we said our good-byes to the Browns, after expressing our gratitude for all of their hospitality. Walking down to the dock with us, Bern said, "I would like to be going with you." Then, after taking our photos, he added, "Be sure to send me a report of the trip. I'll be waiting to hear from you."

"Will do," I replied. With that, we were underway, paddling west around the tip of the peninsula upon which the settlement and landing strip are located. It had been a perfect day. The surface of the lake was calm as we turned the point of land and headed toward the east shore, with Darrell in the Monarch, and Deb and I in the Wenonah. Loons were whimpering to one another between their prolonged dives beneath the surface. Arctic terns, gulls and ducks chattered and squawked in the distance and occasionally came drifting by. Already we were enjoying the 'Spell of the North.' It was a perfect picture.

For more on the life of Bern Will Brown read his:

Arctic Journal published by Novalis in 1998

Arctic Journal II published by Novalis in 1999

8

The Ross River

Two hours later, with aching arms, we found a fine place to set up our first camp, and soon had tents erected. Darrell and Deb would use his Eureka, and I the old pup tent that the two of us had used while descending the Kazan and Thelon Rivers. Air mattresses were soon inflated, with sleeping bags unrolled inside the tents, at a few minutes before midnight, we began to relax around a friendly campfire. "The sun still shines," I commented, "but it's getting pretty low."

"It must be nearing its lowest point for tonight," Darrell replied. "Bern said that it will next drop below the horizon on July 19."

After giving it a little thought, I replied, "That means, here they have about fifty-six days each summer when the sun doesn't set."

"Yes. I guess so. In that case, there must be fifty-six days around Christmas when the sun never appears above the horizon."

While we sipped on cups of hot chocolate, Deb remarked, "The Browns are certainly nice people."

"Sure are!" Darrell replied.

"Those paintings of Bern's are almost unbelievable," I added. "I don't understand how anyone could ever learn to paint so well."

"Me either!" said Deb. "He certainly is one talented artist. And he's equally good at other things, too. How about all of those log buildings?"

"That is amazing," Darrell replied. "And, I understand the settlement is the only all log cabin village still in use in Northwest Territories. Bern certainly lives an interesting and active life up here."

"I don't understand how any one man can accomplish so much," I added. "He's the missionary to the community and he's a writer. I've read an excellent article he wrote for *The Beaver* about Hareskin Indians. He's also a trapper, a hunter, a photographer and a dog-musher, an aircraft pilot and a member of the Explorers Club."

"Certainly one outstanding man, that's for sure," Deb added. "And Margaret is likewise an amazing woman."

Our discussion of the Browns and the day's happenings continued until nearly 1:00 in the morning. Finally, after writing in our journals, we called it a day.

A strong wind picked up out of the northwest within the next couple of hours. Making an early morning scientific sleeping bag analysis of the weather, we could hear heavy surf crashing onto the sandy shore. When we finally rolled out in mid-forenoon, the temperature stood at 45°. The gray lake was covered with whitecaps. Rain was falling along the opposite side of the lake. Colville is a body of water that lies at eight hundred feet above sea level. It is twenty-five miles long and fifteen miles in width, with its outlet in the northeast corner. Our plan was to follow the eastern shore to the outlet, but we were wind-bound and would not be able to proceed until there was some change.

A campfire was soon going again for warmth and, following breakfast we went for a walk to explore along the shore and back to a small marshy lake. As it turned out, what we should have been doing was installing the spray cover on the Wenonah. We had put the cover on the Monarch earlier, so Darrell could get out and dip a kettle of water for coffee and dishes. Later, with snacks for lunch, we each enjoyed a cup or two of Labrador tea, a hot drink that is easy to prepare. One needs a pot of hot water, into which you drop the new growth from the tips of the Labrador tea plants. Two-thirds of a cup of loosely packed new growth is plenty for a two-quart pot of tea. Let it simmer for about five minutes and you have a delicious hot beverage.

By mid-afternoon the velocity of the wind began to drop. We decided to break camp. Soon a gentle breeze was blowing from the southwest and, as we shoved off, Darrell continued, "We should be able to make it to the outlet before midnight with that nice breeze helping us along." But that was not to be. Within fifteen minutes after launch, the wind suddenly swung back into the northwest. Now, with increasing velocity, spray from the whitecaps began splashing over us from the portside. Darrell, in the Monarch, was having fun, riding over and through the waves. The troughs between the crests continued to grow deeper and deeper. At times, he would drop completely out of sight, except for his head, before again riding back up and over the ensuing roller.

Deb and I struggled on for two or three miles as water continued to build up inside the Wenonah. "Darrell," I shouted, "we can't take too much more of this! Do you suppose we will soon come to a break in the shoreline where we can pull in?"

Glancing at the map in its waterproof envelope held on the deck in front of him with an expansion cord, he called back, "There's no sign of any bays, islands or peninsulas anywhere along here."

"We have to get to shore soon," I yelled. "We'll have to run in on that beach up there."

"O.K.," came the reply. "We're not making much progress anyway, quartering into this gusty wind."

We soon turned downwind, heading for an open beach. "Be prepared to hit the beach running," I called to Deb. "And pull the canoe as far up as you can."

"Ready in the bow!" came the reply.

Three more powerful strokes and a huge wave broke over the stern just before we hit shore, soaking me from the neck down. Jumping into the surf, just as the bow touched bottom, both of us pulled but there was no way to budge the canoe with its load of water. Throwing the paddles ashore, rapidly we grabbed packsacks and equipment, moving them up on the beach. About then, Darrell arrived and within a couple minutes, the worst was over but all hands were soaked. Quickly Darrell moved up into the trees to find a place out of the wind. Shortly he had a fire going as Deb and I rounded up more dry fuel. Soon the tents were up and we all put on dry clothing in an attempt to keep warm. A little later, glancing at the thermometer, the mercury stood at 42°. The campfire was our constant companion that evening as we reorganized and began to dry our wet gear.

Wind velocity dropped overnight. We were up and out of camp before eight the next morning. It was good to be moving north again. This time, however, both spray covers were in place, where they would remain. We had decided to each have a turn in the Monarch, and this was my day.

It was a fine day to be on the lake. Pushing along about one hundred yards off shore, I noticed a large spruce stump that had been sawed off about twelve feet above the ground. Several green branches remained on the stump below the cut.

"Look at that tall stump over there," I called, pointing to the right.

"Wow!" said Deb. "That one must have been cut by a tall Hareskin."

"Bern must have cut that tree in the winter while standing on top of a snow bank," Darrell replied. "And the northeast wind could easily build up a ten foot snowbank where it drifts over that steep slope, just behind."

Around 1:30 in the afternoon, we thought we saw an Indian encampment but as shore was about a half mile to starboard, we continued on. We could also distinguish three upturned canoes. An hour later, while taking a leg stretcher, after rounding a point, the six girls from Minnesota arrived. It had been their camp we passed. We exchanged 'Hello's!' with them from two or three hundred feet away. Pulling on their ponchos just as rain began to fall, they continued on toward the outlet. We did likewise, trailing along behind. They were paddling with power and within a few minutes had disappeared around an island.

Before five we arrived at the vacant outpost camp of Colville Lake Lodge. It was time for another shore break. Stepping up on the dock, we were promptly attacked by three arctic terns. Those birds were certainly unhappy to see us, scolding all the while and diving, time after time. They struck our heads with force enough to knock our hats off. Their attack continued all the while we remained near the dock. "There is no question," said Darrell, "those birds have a nest nearby."

On a hill, just behind Bern and Margaret's fine log cabin outpost camp, a United States flag flew from the top of the tall flagpole. We puzzled over that all evening, wondering why a U.S. flag was flying there.

With more bumps on our heads by the terns, we soon moved on, leaving Colville Lake. Suddenly we were in a fast flowing stream and, within a mile, were shooting our first white water. The Ross River was a delightful change. It appeared to be alive with fish. Grayling were surfacing at every ripple. Ducks and solitary sandpipers were now scolding as we moved through their territory. Bonaparte gulls were feeding on the small fry. In all, there were about three miles of excellent canoeing before entering Ketaniatue Lake. There the rain really began to fall.

We had been looking for a campsite but could find nothing. Finally, I sighted a hill along the northwest shore. Deciding to check it out, I scooted across the lake and found an old Hareskin camp near the hilltop and we soon settled in for some rest as steady rain continued to fall.

The weather kept us in camp until mid-afternoon the next day. Two downpours hit while we paddled the remaining twelve miles of Ketaniatue (the name comes from the Hareskin translation meaning 'the narrows lake'). Paddling through the narrows near mid-lake, we observed a bald eagle and a pair of whistling swans. With the inclement weather continuing, we again set up camp at the extreme east end of Ketaniatue, as we were not eager to battle rapids in the rain. Our map showed that, in the next two and one-half miles, the Ross drops twenty-three feet before flowing into Lugentenue (frozen fish lake), giving us an indication of the strength of those rapids.

With great anticipation the next morning, we entered the river and cautiously were sucked into the fast water. Much to our surprise, we sped around bend after bend, with Darrell leading the way in the Monarch. The river water level was high and all conditions were perfect including the scenery as a brown bear scurried up over the right riverbank. Then on a gravel bar at a sharp bend to the right, a big tan wolf stood looking at us. We were so busy on the paddles that it was impossible to shoot a picture without crashing into the gravel bar. Then swinging back to the left, a white wolf ran up the riverbank and looked back at us. In less than ten minutes, we had descended the swoosher and entered Lugentenue.

Rounding a peninsula after entering the lake, more whistling swans appeared. Solitary sandpipers were nesting on every point and island as we moved across the lake.

Below Lugentenue it was another twenty miles of the Ross, much of which is a swift stream, alive with wildlife. There were more bald eagles, terns and gulls feeding on the fish. An otter put on a show for us. At each riffle families of ducks appeared as the mother often tried her broken wing trick, attempting to lure us away from the ducklings.

Camping time found us on a point of land near the outlet of an unnamed lake where the river turns south for a couple of miles. This is where we learned from experience, that it is unwise to camp in a territory claimed by a solitary sandpiper. The bird remained within forty feet of us, continuing its shrill and noisy *weet-weet-weet-weet* all night long.

Just before entering Sokatue Lake, we again encamped near the foot of an esker along the left side of the river. Following supper, it was a two-mile walk along the esker and from up there the scene was magnificent. Looking to the northwest across Sokatue, we could see the old and deserted Hareskin settlement of Soka and the river channel winding its way on west into Niwelin Lake.

Back in camp a weasel scurried along the riverbank, and returned a few minutes later with head held high, carrying a brown lemming in its mouth. Common loons were even more vocal than normal. "Those birds must be trying to tell us something. If I understand them correctly," I said, "we can expect a rough and windy day tomorrow."

"That's the way it sounds," Deb replied.

A strong wind from the northwest flapped and rattled the tents throughout the night and a blowing snowstorm was in progress as we rolled out next morning. The temperature stood at 32°. Right after breakfast, it was back into the sacks for protection from the cold.

Loons were plentiful along the Ross River

The wind-chill factor was hovering between zero and five above. By lunchtime in mid-afternoon, the mercury had risen to 34° and the snow showers had moved elsewhere. It was impossible to keep warm by the roaring campfire, so we were soon once more inside our sleeping bags with our clothes on.

In the evening we heard an aircraft. Sticking our heads out of the tent flaps, we discovered a Cessna 185 circling around. Before we could get out of the tents, it had splashed down in the river in front of camp. Nosing in toward the bank, the plane's door opened and a man called out, "Are you the Klein party?"

"Yes," I answered, hoping it was not some bad news from home.

"Would you come down here?" the man continued. "There's someone on the radio who wants to talk with you."

Sliding down the steep twenty-foot sandbank to the river, I shook hands with Reggie Pfeifer. He had been sent in by Bern to make sure we were all okay. I chatted with Bern for a few minutes on the radio. He also asked about the progress of the six girls. I replied, "We think they are somewhere ahead of us. They passed us near the outlet of Colville Lake and we haven't seen anything of them since." Thanking Bern for checking on us, Mr. Pfeifer snapped off the radio.

There were two passengers in the plane, a father and son, Eric and Stuart Bodtker of Midway, British Columbia. The pilot and owner of the Cessna, Reggie Pfeifer, was from Victoria, B.C. The three came up the bank to meet Deb and Darrell, who by that time had another fire blazing. Trying to keep warm, we visited and sipped hot coffee. The three were on holiday to do some fishing. Their report was 'lots of lunkers,' wherever they tried. They were soon ready to leave in an attempt to locate the six girls, before returning to their fishing camp on some unknown lake.

The temperature had risen to 40° as we took a few snacks, including a handful of gorp, and crawled back into the tents as the wind howled on. This had been our first 'zero' day of progress.

Early the next morning the wind velocity was more reasonable and came out of the west. With a good start under cold, gray skies we crossed Sokatue and slid down the three miles of river into Niwelin Lake. By then we were facing another rising wind. Digging ahead to the west, eventually we turned north keeping just offshore, riding parallel to the waves. Frequently water rolled across the spray covers. Arriving at the narrows, we could find no place to safely take a much needed shore break, so we struggled on, finally completing the two-mile crossing to the western shore.

It was Deb's day in the Monarch. We were all pretty well beat but it was so good to have the shoreline protect us from the wind that we continued on to Niwelin's outlet. There, for the first time, Darrell strung up his fishing rod to secure a fish for supper. Hooking a laker on the first cast, we put it on the stringer.

Within ten minutes, he had caught two more and Deb one. That's where we called a halt to the fishing. Those trout were of uniform size, each weighing in between five and six pounds. Certainly all the fish we could possibly use in the next few days.

It had been a long and difficult day of paddling into the wind. We were not only tired, but also hungry and ready to find a campsite. The area around the outlet of Niwelin is low and marshy. We decided to set up camp at the first opportunity and have our fish fry. "Surely," said Darrell, "we'll find a spot down near the falls."

"That would be cool. Whoops! I didn't mean that. I'm cold enough right now," Deb replied. "But it will be great to camp near those falls."

We kept moving along, and within three minutes could hear the throaty roar of the waterfall ahead. As we approached, we watched closely for either a campsite or some sign of trail leading around the falls. There was nothing, not even a blaze on a tree. The river narrowed but sped between rock walls, disappearing from view. Our map showed that the Ross swings to the right a short distance below the falls, so at the last possible moment we put ashore to starboard. Pulling the canoes up into the willows, we each shouldered a pack. Carrying something in each hand and in a single file, we started up over a knoll. Trees and brush were extremely thick. No trail could be found, but the line of least resistance led us away from the river as the roar of the falls faded in the distance. The far side of the knoll turned out to be a sheer rock bluff with a drop of about sixty feet. By going still farther from the river, we managed to work our way to the foot of the cliff. There we crossed a brushy ravine and climbed up over another ridge of rocks while heading back to the river. At the start, Darrell had been leading the way with me close behind, while Deb brought up the rear. Now, however, I found myself bringing up the rear and even having difficulty keeping my two kids in sight. I was beat! Finally we arrived at the river and dropped our loads.

"We made a mistake," said Darrell as he bent down to dip a cup full of water from the river. "The trail has to be on the other side." Deb and I also enjoyed a cold drink from the cup as we caught our breath, and Darrell continued. "It's impossible to bring the canoes down through all the tangle of brush and over those bluffs. Let's pile our gear here where it will show from across the river, then go back to the canoes, cross the river and look for a trail over there."

"Sounds like our best bet," I replied.

Retracing our footsteps back to the canoes, we soon nosed out into the current. By paddling with power upstream, we were able to ferry across the river and work our way into the willows hanging out from the left bank. Soon, Darrell was scouting for the trail along the edge of the hill. "Maybe this is it," he called.

"I don't see a trail but here's some old axe marks on a stump."

Unloading the remaining gear, we pulled the canoes out of the water and started over what may have been an ancient and seldom used trail. It was rough going! Again, the trail led us well away from the river, and even though we were on high ground, the terrain was a wet, spongy muskeg everywhere. We sank halfway to our knees with nearly every step. In reality it was not a trail, but eventually we managed to pick our way through the forest and back to the river's edge at a place where we could see our packs piled on the opposite side of the river.

Returning to pick up the empty canoes, the stringer of trout and the remaining gear, we tried to find a shorter route by following the high, rocky ledge near the river. It proved to be impossible as a tangle of trees, deadfalls and brush prevented us from even getting close to the edge of the cliff. Much to our disappointment, we never did manage to get a peek at those falls.

There was no suitable campsite anywhere in the vicinity. While Darrell and Deb took the Wenonah across the river to pick up the gear, I loaded the Monarch. Finally at twenty minutes after ten, we shoved off down river, desperately needing a campsite and some supper. We descended another three or four miles of fast flowing river and entered the grassy, weedy bay at the south of Gassend Lake. Still we found no place to camp. Low, bushy tundra was all we could see. It was in desperation that we finally climbed up on a soggy bank of peat moss a few feet above the lake and set up the tents.

Cleaning the four trout, three of which we boiled for future meals, took extra time. At midnight we were eating supper under heavily overcast skies. The temperature had risen to 48 degrees, bringing out the insects in full force. With our camp in a muskeg bog, and no trees for protection from the wind, little did we know what we were in for. Rain set in before morning. The downpour continued until 3:00 in the afternoon. Then a quick breakfast of coffee, an orange and a cup of oatmeal. That was it for the day as rain soon returned and the strong northwest wind whipped on. The temperature had been 38° in the morning, but continued to fall as the day progressed. The only place to keep warm and dry was inside the sleeping bags.

Saturday morning, July 20, I rolled out well rested at 5:15 thinking we might possibly pack up and move out of our miserable bog, but I stepped into winter. There was more than an inch of wet snow covering everything and more windblown snow was coming at us. The temperature stood at 31°, so it was back into the sack once more. Shortly after 9:00 the storm began to subside. We were out for our first substantial meal since Thursday evening's fish dinner. Wind velocity began to taper off and we soon broke camp to paddle the six miles north to the outlet of Gassend Lake. While doing so, we crossed the 68th parallel. There

Darrell shoots a drop in Ross River

are several fine beaches in the vicinity of the outlet, which would have made excellent campsites.

Re-entering the river, we were again in picturesque country. The Ross is certainly a beautiful, wild, free flowing river. It was rapids after rapids around every bend. A pair of peregrine falcons was nesting in some cliffs. We enjoyed and photographed a mother loon with a baby on her back and another white tundra wolf. There were more swans, ducks, terns and eagles. We were able to canoe right down into the Anderson River by 5:00 in the afternoon and an hour later found a good campsite in a clump of trees. Rain showers continued off and on throughout the day but it seemed much warmer in those trees. We had taken nine days to descend the 148 miles of the Ross River. In that distance, there was only one portage required and we had dropped 360 feet nearer to sea level.

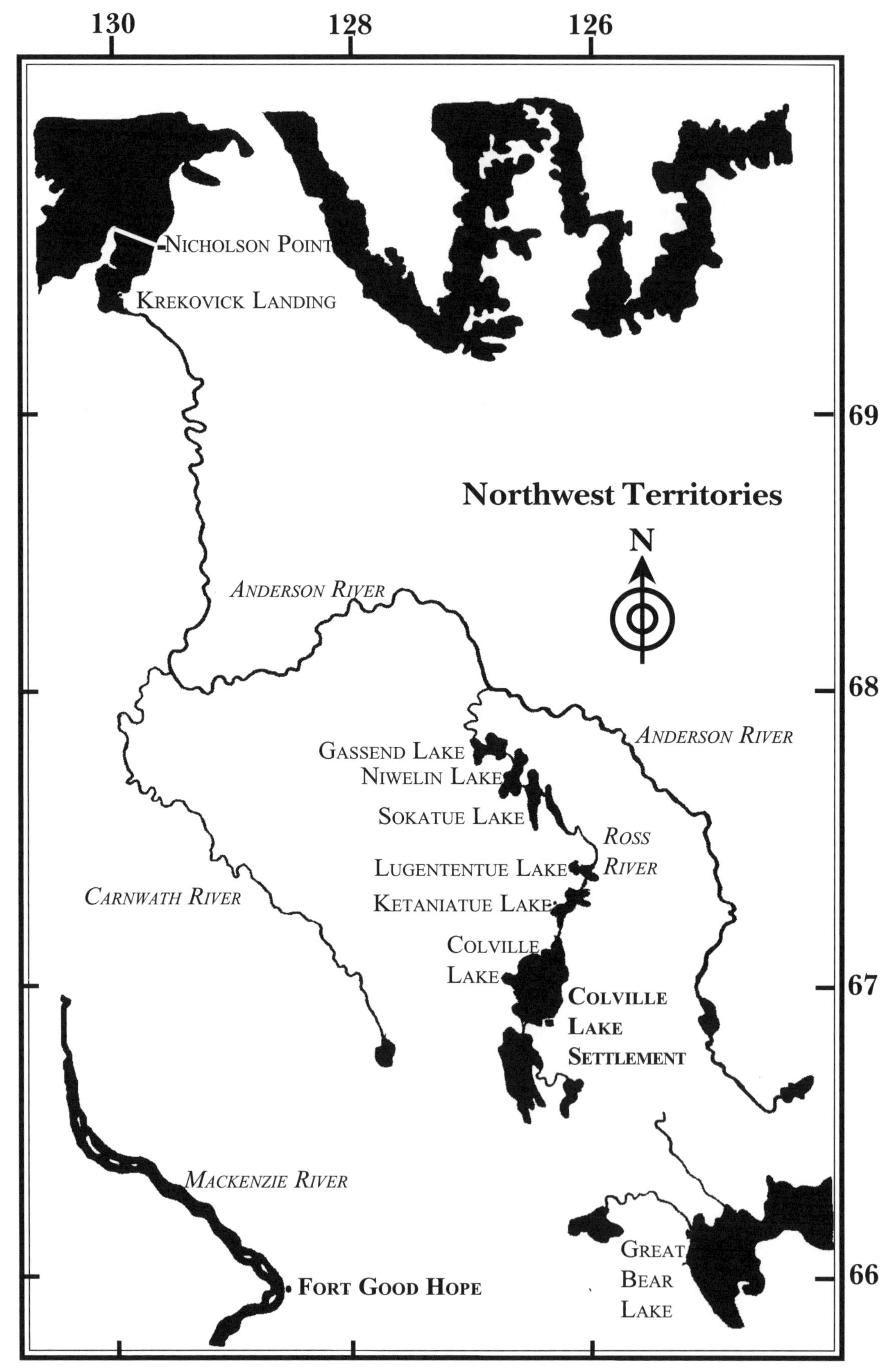
130
128
126
69
68
67
66
Nicholson Point
Krekovick Landing
Northwest Territories
N
Anderson River
Anderson River
Gassend Lake
Niwelin Lake
Sokatue Lake
Ross River
Lugententue Lake
Ketaniatue Lake
Carnwath River
Colville Lake
Colville Lake Settlement
Mackenzie River
Fort Good Hope
Great Bear Lake

9

The Anderson River

The Anderson more than doubles in size below its confluence with the Ross. Now we were on a sizeable river. With the rain still falling, we slept in on Sunday morning. By noon the mercury stood at 36°. With breakfast out of the way, we headed on even though intermittent showers persisted.

An interesting limestone ledge soon appeared, bringing us to Sulfur Rapids. After looking it over, we decided to make a short portage on the left. It may have been possible to shoot this one or line it down but we wanted to 'play it safe.'

Several other drops occur within the next few miles. Stopping above each to look them over, each time we were able to shoot through successfully. We relied heavily on Darrell, a proven expert at reading a river. He led the way in the Monarch. We would watch for his signal as to whether a rapids looked shootable, "so follow me," or "we'd better stop and look this one over."

"Rain keeps getting on my glasses," he said, "it impairs my vision. I tried it with my glasses off, but I can't see very well that way either."

"It's difficult on such a dark, rainy day," I replied. "Sure hope it clears up soon. The thought of entering Falcon Canyon in this poor visibility really worries me." Nor did we relish the thought of being caught in the canyon and not being able to find a campsite.

Paddling down the Anderson River

Moving on, we soon arrived at the final bend above the canyon. There we decided to camp. It had rained all afternoon and, with the 36° to 40° temperatures, we were cold, wet and miserable.

"Maybe," I said as we unloaded the canoes, "we'll have a sunny day tomorrow."

"Let's hope so," Deb replied. "We need more light than this if we're going to get good pictures of this stupendous scenery."

"It's impossible to properly read the rapids in such poor light," Darrell added.

A roaring campfire and a good supper dispelled the gloom. The rain stopped falling and we were soon drying our wet pants, boots and socks near the fire. This was becoming an almost daily ritual. Each evening around the blaze, we would drive stakes and turn wet boots upside down over the stakes. Then it was a matter of turning the boots from side to side to keep them from burning while the heat dried them. Socks and gloves steamed as they also dried near the fire. Sleeping equipment was carried inside plastic liners in the packs and was only aired when conditions were favorable.

While holding a pair of socks to dry near the blaze, Darrell said, "Those girls must be miles ahead of us by now. I'm wondering if we'll ever catch them. Nine days have passed since they disappeared ahead of us in Colville Lake. Maybe we passed them in one of those big lakes on the Ross."

The next morning, under heavily overcast skies and 36° of temperature, we entered Falcon Canyon. The Anderson drops thirty-two feet within four miles as it swirls down the canyon. Continuing our regular procedure of walking ahead to scout each drop before proceeding, we moved forward. Only one time did we choose to make a short portage over a rocky ledge. The canyon continually bends one way or the other with rapids around every curve. Sheer cliffs drop to the water's edge and the scenery was indeed 'stupendous.' Peregrine falcons nesting on high ledges along the rock walls circled overhead, uttering their alarming call.

At 1:30, shooting down some fast water where the canyon bends to the left, we came upon three upturned canoes on the rocky shore. Swinging around in the eddy below, we put ashore. There were the six young ladies. One named Maude Patnode, the 25-year-old group leader, had just rolled out. She soon told us that a girl named Kim Benson had nearly drowned in the fast water there on Saturday evening. They had been lining their canoes down the rapids that we had just shot, and Kim, on the stern rope, was swept off her feet into the frigid torrent. They had fished her out of the eddy below and set up camp right there. Rapidly they put her into some dry clothing and sleeping bag, but by then the cold water had taken its toll. She went into hypothermic shock. "We worked over her and did body to body warming in the sleeping bag. Eventually we got her warmed up." Maude continued, "But we had to lay over another day."

"How is she now?" I asked.

"She's all right again and we're soon going to break camp."

We chatted briefly, then shoved off and soon broke out of the canyon, but still had plenty of interesting river, with several riffles and rapids to negotiate. There was a short portage just before the river makes its major turn to the west.

Then, hearing a plane, we looked up and it was Reggie Pfeifer heading directly at us. Skimming past only thirty or forty feet above our heads, he continued on south where the six young ladies would certainly be in view.

Three miles to the west we camped above a high bank on the left. It had been a good day on the river even though overcast, cold and windy. While drying boots and socks, Darrell reported, "We progressed twenty-two miles and have descended another 145 feet nearer to sea level since morning."

Sometime around midnight, peeking out of the tents, we saw three canoes with the young women moving down the river.

Miraculously, the next morning the sun was shining in a picture book sky. It would be a great day for canoeing. Around noon we quietly passed the tent camp, with the three upturned canoes but no sign of life. When we were well down river, Deb turned and, speaking with a grin said, "The girls will probably think we are still behind them."

"They certainly do like to sleep in," I replied. Three hours later we arrived at the Limestone Steps, which are a series of rapids and a waterfall as the river swings first to the right and then to the left. Here, mosquitoes and black flies gave us a real workout. They must have been especially hungry as they attacked relentlessly. We moved the packs and canoes across nearly a mile-and-a-quarter of tundra to a backwater below the falls. This was the longest portage along the way and two-and-a-half hours later we were able to shove off down river once more. Then came still more shootable rapids and, to close out the day's exciting run, we enjoyed chasing a molting swan down river for several miles. The bird kept up a continuing "squawk" at nearly every stroke of our paddles, but never once attempted to go ashore.

Wednesday, July 24 dawned bright and clear. In the first hour we lined down and portaged Flatrock Rapids where the river drops over another limestone ledge, with high hills on either side.

Lunchtime found us enjoying gorgeous scenery at a place known as the Limestone Towers where a pair of nesting peregrine falcons entertained us. Later, passing a gravel bar, we startled a bull caribou with huge antlers. Jumping to his feet, he splashed to shore through shallow water.

Bern Will Brown had told us to watch for a fossil bluff on the right. We took a leg stretcher at the place he had marked on our maps. It was most impressive. The entire bluff, more than a hundred feet in height and at least a quarter mile long, is gradually eroding into the river. The entire hill is one gigantic pile of sea fossils, which were once at the bottom of a tropical sea. For the next thirty minutes we entertained ourselves searching for small pieces to carry home with us. Looking closely we found the bluff to be made up of several varieties of coral, clam shells and numerous other varieties, all fossilized and held in place by permafrost. For our collection, we scratched out a number of complete tiny clams, petrified in their shells.

Several miles downstream we set up camp on a flat rock ledge as another storm headed out way. The place was about five miles upstream of Juniper Rapids. Huge, eroded, gravelly hillsides towered above on both sides adding to the solitude.

Rain set in shortly after we crawled into the sacks and continued until breakfast time. Popping out, we quickly broke camp as everything was soaking wet and getting wetter on the flat rock ledge. The rain persisted as we moved down to Juniper Rapids. Darrell looked it over and reported, "We can shoot it but will have to thread the needle, hitting it in precisely the right spot, just to the right of the big rock."

He led the way in the Monarch and we followed only about eighty feet behind. He disappeared over the first drop, then shot along the edge of a couple of subsequent standing waves. Deb and I were already committed. There was no turning back in the rushing surge. Sliding to the right of the big rock, I realized the bow was slightly too far to the left. "Draw right!" I yelled. Shooting over the drop, we were unable to bring the bow back to the precise heading, and crash! The Wenonah shuddered and slid, scraping over the lower ledge and right into the center of a huge standing wave. The spray cover was what saved the day for us as we floundered through the standing waves and scraped over another rock. We had survived!

The rain refused to let up and we were unable to find a place to set up a shelter. Moving on, the three of us were soaking wet, cold and hungry. Finally, in early afternoon, we could take no more. Climbing a steep bank, we hacked out a little spot between two black spruces and put up a tarp for shelter. Soon, in front of our makeshift lean-to, Darrell had a fire going. For the next couple of hours we hugged the fire standing under the edge of the tarp, trying to warm ourselves, dry wet clothing and take on a little food. Even though I had worn my rain suit the entire time, my jacket and shirt were dripping wet when I took them off.

A couple of hours later we were up to moving on in hopes of finding a decent camping place, even though lighter showers now prevailed. On downstream, wolves howled in the distance. Later, four of them watched from a hillside as we passed below.

The skies once more began to clear as we set up camp on another huge gravel bar. Drying our wet things required several hours as the welcome fire consumed piles of fuel. Following a big supper, Darrell baked a loaf of corn meal bread. We also devoured half of that, along with butter, while it was still hot.

Lounging around the fire, we discussed our situation. Our original plan was to paddle into Tuktoyaktyuk after crossing Liverpool Bay. Two weeks had passed since leaving Colville Lake and it was still another 160 miles to Krekovick Landing at the mouth of the Anderson.

"As far as I'm concerned," Darrell said, "I would just as soon terminate this trip when we get to the Canadian Wildlife Service cabin at Krekovick Landing, if there's anyone around."

"Sounds good to me," I replied.

"Me, too," Deb responded. "I will have had plenty of canoeing by then. Somewhere it has to be summer. I'm anxious to get there and warm up these cold feet of mine."

"If the Ranger isn't at the station when we get to Krekovick," Darrell continued, "we can paddle on out to the Dew Line station at Nicholson Point. That's only another twenty-two miles. A day's travel if the weather is good."

Friday was another very fine day. "Maybe we're finally going to have a streak of good weather," Darrell said, as he rolled the tent.

"Could be," I replied. "We're certainly due for a break."

"That'll bring out the insects," Deb added, "but I prefer insects to what we've been having."

Maintaining a steady pace, by noon we were passing the confluence with the Carnwath River, one of the Anderson's major tributaries. The hills along this section of the river reach up to six hundred feet in many places.

Small groups of caribou grazed and trotted along the shores. Whistling swans again swam ahead leading us down river. Red-throated and Arctic loons entertained us, flying along and splashing down on the water in the distance.

Basking in the sun as we paddled along was truly enjoyable. Suddenly the John Denver tune 'Sunshine on My Shoulders' came to mind. Little by little we recalled the words. Soon, with canoes in close proximity, we were singing—

'Sunshine on my shoulders makes me happy
Sunshine in my eyes can make me cry
Sunshine on the water looks so lovely
Sunshine almost always makes me high.'

Camping time found us setting up near a padlocked Canadian Water Resources shack, to enjoy another period of rest and relaxation. It had been a 70° day and the only time during the entire journey when it warmed to more than 58°. We had progressed another thirty-eight miles.

More rain was falling as we headed out the next morning and continued until early afternoon. The high point of the day came when we located the ruins of old Fort Anderson atop a fifty-foot gravel bank on the east side of the river. The entrance to the Fort, still traceable on the ground, is about forty feet from the present eroded riverbank, with only a few decaying timbers visible. The outline of the picket palisades still shows at each of the four corners. The perimeter of the old Fort was 125 feet across the front and about 115 feet along its sides. Fort Anderson was built during the summer of 1861 by the Hudson's Bay Company, under the direction of Roderick MacFarlane, who was then manager of the Company's post at Fort Good Hope. From here, the Company served the Hareskins from the south and Eskimos from the north. In 1864, following the death of sixty-four sled dogs due to distemper and the death of many Eskimo hunters due to a major outbreak of scarlet fever in 1865, the Fort was closed. Small black spruce trees and grass interspersed with fireweed now grow where Fort Anderson once stood.

An hour after leaving the historical site, the rain let up and a strong northwest wind soon picked up to gale force. With the river flowing toward the driving wind, we had our work cut out for us. Within an hour, further progress became impossible. We were blown off the river on an island where we were forced to wait out the cold summer wind. Huddling around our fire, we watched as a gray wolf trotted along the shoreline.

A few ruins of trappers' cabins still stand near the river, one of which came into view the following morning as we moved on. The wind had died while we slept so we were out early in 36° temperature.

Before noon we crossed the 69th parallel. Several groups of caribou were again seen moving along, most of which swam across the river. By pushing along until eight in the evening, we set up camp at Windy Bend. Then came more rain and it was noon next day by the time we completed Windy Bend. There, as our old nemesis, the cold north wind, whipped up the river with thirty mile per hour gusts, we realized that Windy Bend was indeed well named.

Caribou were becoming more and more plentiful. On our earlier journeys, we had paddled through the Beverly and Bathurst herds of barren land caribou. Now, however, we were in the territory of the Bluenose herd. Nearly every time we came upon a group moving along the shore, they would look us over, then run ahead and attempt to swim across the river. Consequently, we learned that by paddling with power toward a group, we could often move right in amongst them. Many groups were small while others contained more than a hundred animals. At times, as they crossed the river, we would zero in on a single bull or a small group and chase them ashore. At other times, we would maneuver in close enough to slap them on the rump with a paddle. It was good fun! Had we

Pushing caribou across the Anderson River

been hunting, it would have been 'duck soup' or, in this case, 'caribou soup.' It was easy to see how, before firearms, the native peoples could paddle their kayaks right up to these animals and spear them as they swam the rivers.

The barren hills along the lower Anderson range up to six and seven hundred feet above the river. At both Windy and Husky Bends, those hills are brilliantly colored, with slopes of various colors ranging from reds to yellow to white and even lavender.

In the afternoon more groups of molting swans paddled down river ahead of us. At times, if we moved too close, there would be a great flapping of wings combined with splashing water as these great white birds attempted to run along the surface. Seldom would they gain more than a hundred yards on our canoes, before once more settling back into the water. We were traveling through the major nesting area in North America of those magnificent birds.

As we scooted past the end of an island, a large barren ground grizzly wandered along the shore and up into the bushes.

Evening found us trying to find a campsite in Husky Bend. Finally, we set up beside a little stream flowing out of the high and colorful hills on the right. Dipping a kettle of water from the stream for cooking, I tasted it. The water was very strongly acid, impossible for either cooking or drinking. "This stream must flow out of a sulfur pit," I told Darrell, offering him a taste. "But be careful! Don't swallow any!"

He took a slight sip. "Wow! It is sour!" Spitting and throwing the dilute sulfuric acid out, Darrell took the kettle and headed for the big river for some fresh water we could use. With the cold north wind blowing in off the Arctic Ocean, we had a problem keeping warm, even while huddling near the fire. With no insect problem and a real nip in the air, we went for a long walk up and across those picturesque hills before crawling into the sacks.

Fog had settled in and the thermometer showed 32° the next morning. Heading west out of colorful Husky Bend, the fog began to lift, revealing a clear, blue sky. "It's thirty-six miles to Krekovick Landing," said Darrell, "and there's a chance we might make it before setting up camp again."

"Let's give it our best shot," I replied. "Possibly there's an aircraft in there right now."

"With our luck, it will probably be flying away just before we arrive," Deb added. The three of us were eager to get back to civilization. It seemed our passion for the wilderness had been fully satisfied for at least a few weeks.

Caribou herds were almost everywhere along the way. Most were bulls, yearlings and two-year-olds. No cows or calves were detected. The mature females and calves still hadn't returned from the calving grounds. Many of the bulls carried huge racks of antlers. They appeared to be darker in color, and somewhat

The author on the shoreline of the Arctic Ocean

larger animals than those Darrell and I had seen in the Beverly and Bathurst herds, during our descents of the Thelon and Back Rivers. Group after group would look us over, run ahead and invariably swim across the river. They were a joy to watch.

A stiff breeze from the north picked up before noon and continued throughout the day, impeding our progress. About twenty miles short of the ocean, we discovered we were paddling in tidal waters. First, there was no river current moving our way, then we were pushing against an incoming tide. Our work was cut out for us, and especially so if we were to reach the Canadian Wildlife Service cabin that day.

With aching arms and bottoms, we stopped for a speedy supper as huge caribou antlers moved along above the dwarf vegetation. Then it was on toward the river mouth, as it widens out into the delta. Piles of driftwood lined the shores. Hanging in there persistently, we finally arrived at Krekovick Landing and had our first look at the Arctic Ocean at a half-hour before midnight. We had completed the descent of the Ross and Anderson Rivers in nineteen days.

Pulling the canoes ashore over the pebbly beach, we headed up the steps to the white CWS cabin. A heavy board was propped against the entrance; a solid wooden door with rows of spikes protruding about three inches. Other spikes with points extended were around the windows, the edge of the roof and corners of the bear proof cabin. There was no one around so we soon found a level place down near the shore, erected the tents, and build a cheerful fire from the piles of driftwood. It was hot chocolate time. Then at 1:00 in the morning, we called it a day.

Darrell was out early. He decided to have a look around inside the CWS cabin. In a little while he reported that he had found a two-way battery powered radio inside. He had snapped it on and apparently it was in working order. With that news, I was soon up there to check it out. We had no idea what the radio was tuned to but could hear someone talking to an aircraft flying over Victoria Island. When a lull in the conversation occurred, I held down the mike switch and had a go at it. "This is Krekovick Landing. Do you read?" Then, after repeating it again, a man's voice replied.

"Go ahead Krekovick Landing."

"There are three of us in the Klein party. We request that you contact Aklak Air in Inuvik, and ask them to dispatch an aircraft here to fly us back to their base. Over."

"Is this an emergency? Over."

"Negative."

"Are you short of food? Over."

"Negative. We have canoed down the Anderson River and need transportation to Inuvik."

"I'll see what we can do," the voice replied.

"Thank you very much. Over and out." With that, I snapped off the radio.

Good news! We enjoyed a big breakfast, leisurely washed and packed the cook kit and everything else except the tents. We would leave those up until the dew dried off or until we heard an aircraft approaching. Walking back up to the cabin to look around, we found a logbook on the table. The latest entry was dated July 24, seven days earlier and signed by Sam Berry of the Canadian Wildlife Service. The note read, "Upon completion of the Grizzly survey, we estimate the bears in this area have destroyed at least ten thousand swan eggs this spring."

Just after eleven, I decided to use the radio again to learn whether or not the man had been able to get the message through to Aklak Air. This time a different person was at the controls. When I asked the question, he responded. "Where is Krekovick Landing?"

"At the mouth of the Anderson River," I replied.

"Oh! So that's where it is. I'll put your request through right away."

Having more time to kill, I walked along the pebbled tidal flats for about a mile to the north. Moving along, I realized we were at the end of our journey and more than likely this was the farthest north I would get in my lifetime. In a prayerful mood, I thanked God for dozens of things including His seeing us safely to the shores of the Arctic Ocean, and for my two wonderful canoeing companions. Returning to camp, Deb and Darrell were relaxing near the fire. A half-hour later with Deb standing not more than twenty feet from the sea, she and I watched two caribou bulls trotting our way close to the shore. Those animals kept on coming and passed between us and the ocean without ever noticing we were there.

Finally, around three in the afternoon, we heard an aircraft approaching. Sure enough, it was a Cessna 185 from Aklak Air. We tied the Monarch just above the left pontoon, loaded our packs and were soon flying toward Inuvik. The pilot would return during the evening for the Wenonah. We asked him what radio base we had communicated with, to which he replied, "Arctic Shelf Exploration in Tuktoyaktyuk. They were quite upset that you were using their frequency."

Hot showers in the Finto Motor Inn were most welcome as we watched the dirt, built up during three weeks in camp, go down the drain. Then early the next morning we began the long drive back to Michigan.

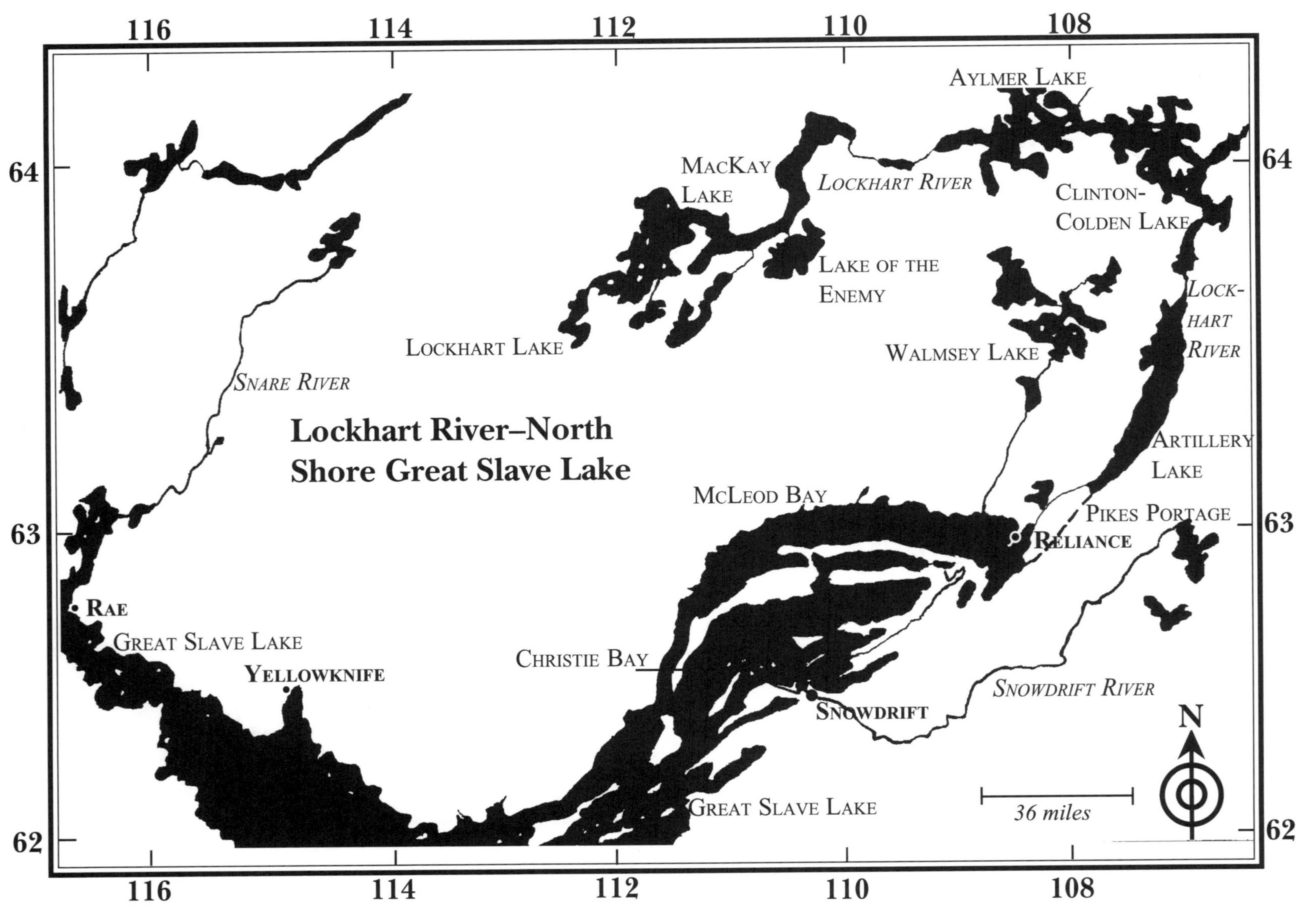
Lockhart River–North
Shore Great Slave Lake
116
114
112
110
108
64
63
62
Aylmer Lake
MacKay
Lake
Lockhart River
Clinton-
Colden Lake
Lake of the
Enemy
Lock-
hart
River
Lockhart Lake
Walmsey Lake
Snare River
Artillery
Lake
McLeod Bay
Pikes Portage
Reliance
Rae
Great Slave Lake
Yellowknife
Christie Bay
Snowdrift River
Snowdrift
N
36 miles
Great Slave Lake

10

Lockhart River

There were still many isolated Canadian rivers waiting to be explored. Time was slipping away. In January of 1989 came some good news. Darrell agreed to join me for a journey down the Lockhart River to Fort Reliance on Great Slave Lake in Northwest Territories.

We had descended the Anderson River using a Mad River Monarch designed by Verlen Kruger. We both had used it on several shorter trips in Ontario and Michigan during the intervening years. It was such a joy to paddle when compared to the Grumman and Wenonah tandem canoes we had previously used. Thus in May we purchased another Monarch. Now we would each have a solo canoe.

This time we would drive to Yellowknife and have La Ronge Airways fly us into Lake of the Enemy, south of McKay Lake. We both went into serious training for the journey. Three times each week during the month of June, I shouldered the Monarch and walked a mile at a time under it. We also carried our backpacks with seventy pounds of rock inside around my woodland trail and also paddled on the nearby Shiawassee River in an attempt to be in peak condition.

A few days prior to departure a strange thing happened. I acquired a persistent headache. This was something unusual for me. A physical exam in the spring showed me to be in excellent health, even though Dr. Chong H. Park had me taking an Ascriptin tablet every second day for a previous heart condition. When departure date came I was not too concerned, thinking the headache would likely be gone in a day or two.

Driving the 2,953 miles to Yellowknife in three and a half days, it was July 4 when we were greeted by Bill Galwitz at La Ronge Airways base. Anticipating our arrival, Bill asked, "Are you ready to go?"

"We still need to secure a travel permit, buy a fishing license and call home," I replied.

"That's all right. We'll load the canoes and we'll be ready whenever you are."

At a sporting goods store in the City Centre we were shocked at the cost of a fishing license. It was $40.00 plus G.S.T. (General Service Tax). This charge certainly didn't help my headache problem. We bought only one for Darrell. He would do the fishing.

By the time we returned to the La Ronge base, the crew helped load our packs in their Twin Otter and we were soon underway. Arriving over Lake of the Enemy our pilot circled the entire lake without seeing a satisfactory place to put us ashore. There was a sandy beach in sight over in McKay, opposite the outlet of Lake of the Enemy. We headed for the beach and once ashore soon found a place to set up our first camp.

Two days of paddling took us to the east end of McKay Lake. Then it was down the Lockhart River with much fast water and rapids after rapids. We did a lot of scouting ahead, made two portages and ran some exciting drops. While scouting past one rough spot in the river we watched a wolverine scurry up and over a bank of snow along the opposite shore.

In addition to the persistent headache, my vision was impaired by a developing cataract in my right eye. We had worked out a system for satisfactory river travel. Darrell would lead the way through difficult places and I would follow about twenty to thirty feet behind. The system was working well until suddenly my canoe became hung up on a rock near the head of a lengthy rapid. Now I was on my own in the rushing torrent. By the time I had stepped out on a slippery rock to pull the canoe into deeper water, Darrell had disappeared around a bend about a third of a mile ahead. I had my work cut out for me, carefully heading on down the shallow boulder field, bumping the occasional rock I didn't see, until it was too late to avoid. Darrell had stopped as soon as he could and was holding onto a big boulder when I pulled up alongside, "Glad to see you made it," he grinned.

Heavy rain moved in as we crossed Lower Outram Lake. We put ashore just above the chute into Aylmer Lake as a powerful cold summer wind suddenly whipped up. Struggling to set up the tent, we crawled inside to try to keep warm, as the cold north wind became a gale. Inside the tent we quickly blew up the air mattress, peeled off the rain gear, put on warm jackets and covered ourselves with sleeping bags in an attempt to keep warm.

"This is about like the weather we experienced along the Back River," said Darrell as he snuggled down under his blanket.

"Certainly is," I replied. "I'm afraid we may have broken our pledge. It's been eleven years since we made our agreement on the north shore of Lower Garry Lake to never, never return for another canoe trip in the arctic barrens, but here we are!"

"This one may blow on past us before morning. Tomorrow could be a fine day."

"Hope so!"

Six hours later the heavy rain let up and the next morning under sunny skies we were underway early. It was to the east all day. Approaching the outlet of Aylmer on July 10, the lake's east end was jammed with pack ice. Detouring around the large island near Thanakoie Narrows and following leads in the pack, we finally squeezed through between floating pans and again entered open water leading down the Narrows. Shortly we entered Clinton-Colden Lake and were given a perfectly calm and sunny day to paddle the thirty-two miles across to a hilltop campsite opposite Tyrrell Point.

Seeking out openings in ice-pack near Thanakoie Narrows

We met Akitoshi Nishimura along the shore of Artillery Lake

Loons, both arctic and red throated, entertained us as we moved along. We heard wolves nearly every day. We made only one portage before entering Artillery Lake. The other sets of rapids below Ptarmigan Lake were all shooters. Then it was on along the west shore of Artillery.

On the morning of July 14 we came upon the camp of Akitoshi Nishimura from Japan. He was paddling solo from Yellowknife to Goa Haven. This was the first person we had seen since the La Ronge pilot who put us ashore in McKay Lake ten days before. Aki (as he likes to be called) asked us questions about his route ahead and he gave us information about things we would encounter along Pikes Portage. Aki had been making lengthy solo canoe trips in northern Canada in each of the recent years.

Heading for the upper end of Pikes Portage the next day, we could hear the throaty roar of the water pouring down the rapids and over Hanbury Falls. The Lockhart plunges down a series of chutes and waterfalls, dropping nearly eight hundred feet in those eighteen miles between Artillery and Great Slave Lakes. This makes canoeing down the river nearly impossible. The feat, however, was accomplished in 1986 by a group headed by George Luste of Toronto.

The twenty-four mile long Pikes Portage consists of a series of portages between eight smaller lakes. The weather was hot each day as we moved along. On July 18 we arrived at the longest carry of Pikes. There are three and one half miles of trail between Harry Lake and Great Slave. Sweating our way across in the 87-degree temperature, in two trips we had moved everything across except the canoes by supper time. Thunder rolled across Great Slave Lake during the evening. Soon the rains came, along with a gale from the northeast. What a storm! The downpour of thunder and lightning, rain, and wind continued until nearly noon of the next day, churning Charlton Bay into froth. Walking back to Harry Lake in the afternoon to carry the canoes across, we were then pushed along by the strong east wind on our return to camp.

Wind velocity had dropped overnight and we paddled the final seven miles to Reliance in a drizzling rain. There at Trophy Lodge we met Lance Luckhart who radioed La Ronge Airways for us. Due to the recent bad weather and their backlog of work, it would be a day or two before they would be able to retrieve us. We asked Lance where we could pitch our tent while waiting.

"Anywhere down around the old D.O.T. would be fine," he replied.

The Department of Transport weather station, a quarter mile to the west, was being phased out in '89. The terrain around it was rough and rocky. There wasn't a level place in sight to set the tent. With blue sky in the north we waited out the day, occasionally talking with interesting people who came our way. One was Roger Catling, the trapper who lives on the point across the little bay. He invited us over for supper but we declined, as there was a chance the La Ronge plane might drop in at any time to pick us up. We were certain that Bill Galwitz would send someone for us as soon as he could. Finally at midnight we set up the tent as best we could on the rocky beach and crawled in.

We walked to Trophy Lodge again the following morning to learn if there was any later word from La Ronge. There we met Richard Black who works with Lance at the Lodge. There was nothing new on our transportation to Yellowknife.

In early afternoon as rain began to fall, a Twin Otter splashed down and taxied to the fuel tanks across the little bay. We assumed they were planning to retrieve us. Quickly packing the tent with rain gear on, we noticed a boat from Trophy Lodge moving passengers from the Otter across to the Lodge. This puzzled us so we paddled over to the fuel depot to learn what was happening. We soon learned that the aircraft had been loaded with fishermen enroute to Lynx Lake Lodge on the upper Thelon. They were turned back due to low visibility and were all having lunch at Trophy.

Standing by the Twin Otter as it refueled, I was visiting with one of the passengers who was from Illinois. I casually quipped, "Be careful in case you see any muskoxen. They can be dangerous. One of them nearly finished me off back in '74 as we descended the Thelon."

Glancing at me, his reply came as a real surprise. "You look to me like the author of a book I recently read. The title of it was ***Cold Summer Wind***. You must be Clayton Klein."

"That's right," I replied. We shook hands and remarked about the coincidence. Now, however, as I write this, regretfully, I do not recall the man's name.

Back at our campsite we waited out the rest of the day. Late in the evening a La Ronge Beaver splashed down to pick us up. By early the next morning we were driving the muddy Mackenzie Highway toward home.

The persistent headache continued to plague me for three more weeks, even though I visited my doctor, Chong H. Park, MD. He, being a cardiologist, sent me to nearby McPherson Hospital for a series of tests including x-rays and an MRI. While waiting for the report on my medical condition, I continued to consume up to a dozen Ascriptin per day to ease the pain. The hospital people could find nothing wrong with me. That was great news, so I suffered on until one day in mid-August. While talking with Verlen Kruger, I mentioned my problem.

"Have you seen your chiropractor about it?" He asked.

"No. Do you think a chiropractor would know anything about a headache?"

"They might," was his reply.

I went directly to see my chiropractor, Dr. Robert Kribs. After telling him of my problem, he laid his hand on my neck and pressing his fingers at the base of my skull, spoke; "There's your problem, right there!" He gave me one adjustment. The headache instantly went away. Best of all, I haven't had even one headache in the twelve intervening years since then.

11

Lower Lockhart–Great Slave Lake

Many times we thought about our trials and tribulations along Pikes Portage. What had we missed by not following the lower Lockhart those final eighteen miles as it plunges down into Great Slave Lake? Darrell and I often discussed the situation as we looked at photos and maps. We really would like to see Anderson Falls where the river drops forty feet, and Parry Falls where it plunges one hundred and thirty feet and Tyrrell Falls with its eighty-five foot descent plus all of the lesser falls between.

We decided to return in 1991. This time we would fly from Yellowknife to the northeast end of Charlton Bay where the Lockhart flows into the Great Slave Lake. We would leave the canoes and most of the camping gear there, then fly on up to a small lake south of Anderson Falls and backpack along the river down to our canoes. Then paddle the north shore of the big lake back to Yellowknife.

It was July 26 when we arrived at the Air Tindi Air Base, late enough so they were unable to fly us in before the next day. Our tents were pitched on a point of land behind the Air Base. It was a noisy night for the two of us. Dozens of aircraft taking off and coming in throughout the wee hours caused us to get little sleep.

The next morning under sunny skies we boarded a turbo Beaver with one of our Monarch canoes securely tied above each float. Pilot Paul Rosset flew us to the mouth of the Lockhart River where we put the canoes and supplies ashore behind a sand beach. A few minutes later we were airborne and flying to the northeast up and over the rapids and waterfalls of the lower Lockhart. Circling between Anderson and Hanbury Falls with Artillery Lake to the east, we decided to have Pilot Paul put us down on a little unnamed lake about a mile south of the river below Anderson Falls.

There, checking compass and map, we slipped on our backpacks and headed north toward the Lockhart. Picking our way along through the rugged mountainous country, we could hear the throaty roar of the river ahead. By mid-day we followed the river down to Parry Falls where the deluge of water drops about twenty feet, turns abruptly 90 degrees to the left and then falls another 110 feet before sliding on down the rock strewn valley.

Then it was downstream for another four hours. In most places, due to the cliffs and steepness of the riverbanks it was impossible to follow along near the shore. The easier backpacking through this boreal forest was usually on the plateau several hundred feet above and well away from the river. Camping overnight on the caribou moss covered plateau was enjoyable. The tinder-dry taiga floor urged caution with the campfire. There was a little creek nearby providing plenty of clear cool drinking water. We built our cooking fire on rocks near the creek and following supper, extinguished the blaze with plenty of water.

Then came another day of rugged backpacking with much up and down hill as we picked our way along through the trackless bush. We passed much whitewater and waterfalls but the best came as we arrived at Tyrrell Falls. There, about 450 feet above a bend in the river and a quarter mile from the torrent we set up camp. What a gorgeous place! Smaller falls both above and below Tyrrell were all visible from our tent sites. The continuing roar coming up out of the canyon was indeed something to behold.

Hiking down to the river's edge we found a place to cook supper where we could dip water as it surged by. On the long climb back up the slope we came upon a bear's den with plenty of fresh sign about.

The third day brought us on down to the sandy beach where we found our canoes and all camping supplies just as we had left them. We were soon stroking the water. A storm was brewing so we quickly paddled to the old Fort Reliance built by Captain George S. Back R.N. in 1833. The rain hit as we arrived so in rain gear we spent an hour looking over the ruins and recent reconstruction of the Fort. Standing under a clump of spruce trees we discussed the scene and the history of the place.

"I guess you know this wasn't really a fort. Fort Reliance was a fort in name only," I remarked. "This place was used to house Capt. Back's crew of men through the winters of 1833 to 1835, while they constructed the boat in which they descended and returned from the river you and I went down in 1978."

"The Back River! I'll never forget that one!" Darrell emphatically replied as the rain poured down. "I recently read an article in *The Beaver* by Margaret Bertirlli. This was the base for Capt. Back's Arctic Land Expedition. He, with a few of his men, struck off from here, up and over the height of land north into the Barrens and located the headwaters of the Great Fish River, as it was then called. By the end of August the party returned here and soon moved into winter quarters that were being constructed by Alexander R. McLeod of the Hudson's Bay Company.

"The winter of 1834 was a rough one around here. In January temperatures plummeted to -70 degrees F. Many of the native people died of the cold weather and starvation. While this was going on Capt. Back and his crew worked up over the ridge near Artillery Lake cutting trees and sawing lumber to build the boat. Then in the spring they hauled their boat north over the ice to begin their descent of the Great Fish River as soon as the river opened."

"During the summer," I interjected, "Back and his crew made it all the way down to Chantry Inlet and returned here for the following winter."

"That's right. I still wonder how they managed to get their big heavy boat down those rapids just below Beechy Lake where the river drops sixty some feet."

"It had to take some skillful maneuvering! That's where you and I made nearly a two mile portage, but I understand those fellows floated it through."

The rain began to let up and a streak of blue appeared through the leaden gray skies, suddenly ending the discussion. We quickly snapped a couple photos and headed for the canoe. Paddling about a mile west crossing Charlton Bay, we carried across the peninsula at its narrowest point.

The next morning under sunny skies we headed west along Great Slave Lake's northeastern arm, McLeod Bay. For safety we chose the Bay's convoluted north shore and would move from point to point as long as weather conditions remained good. There is a steep escarpment along McLeod's south shore and the thought of moving along there could have been a worrisome thing.

Shortly after passing the mouth of the Hoarfrost River, a motorboat came charging out toward us, pulling up alongside. It was David and Kristin Olesen who had lived there in a cabin for the past four years. They invited us in to their place but we declined, wanting to make as many miles as possible while the good weather held. Kristin brought us a loaf of freshly baked rye bread. We chatted for a few minutes before thanking them and saying good-bye.

In 1994 Dave Olesen had a wonderful book published, titled ***North of Reliance***. It's a personal story of his life with Kristin in the wilderness.

Scenery was good along the north shore. One of the highlights is to be found at the mouth of Barnston River. There the Barnston enters McLeod Bay plunging over a twenty-foot waterfall. Another gorgeous place where we camped overnight on bedrock is Sosan Island near the west end of McLeod Bay. That evening we walked up and over the higher part of the island. The scenery was stupendous! We stepped over crevasses up to three feet across and could look down between the huge fragmented rocks more than a hundred feet to the lake surface below. Arctic terns chattered. Rose campion and other arctic flowers grew wherever they could find a footing on those monstrous rocks.

On August 2, approaching The Narrows at the west end of McLeod we came upon Plummer's Great Slave Lake Lodge. Going ashore we met Manager Grant Knowlen and Bill Bliven. Inviting us in, they served Pepsi as they questioned us about our travels. They also asked if we had seen anything of Aki Nishimura, whom they had met on his earlier trips through The Narrows. A few minutes later as we were leaving, both men accompanied us down to the shore, wanting to see our Monarch canoes. Grant handed me a pail of goodies to take along containing a half a dozen bananas and several apples. Great guys!

Headwinds slowed us as we moved south and then west along the north shore of Hearne Channel. Camping over at McKinley Point a couple of nights later, the cruise ship *Norega* rounded our camp and anchored in the little bay only a quarter mile from our tents. A couple of hours later people were walking around our camp with much loud talk. We were sacked out but Darrell exited his tent to chat with some of them and keep an eye on our belongings. Not much sleep for us as the *Norega's* engine dieseled all night long.

Early in the morning on August 7 after camping on one of the larger Cabin Islands, we had a mishap. Launching into heavy surf, as I pulled out into it my canoe flipped over and I fell into Great Slave Lake. What a surprise! Wading ashore where Darrell was still standing with a grin on his face, he helped me pull my Monarch in with it half full of the lake. Most of my packs were floating inside. Unloading everything, we tipped the canoe upside down to drain. I emptied my boots, put on a dry pair of my cleanest dirty socks and loaded up again. My other clothes would dry as I wore them. Thirty minutes after the upset, we launched again. This time I was fully awake and we made it.

A day and a half later we paddled into Yellowknife, ending another enjoyable journey in Northwest Territories.

12

Alaska at Last

Anxiety to paddle overwhelmed me once more in 1993. This time we would head for the Yukon. This would be different. Now we would travel as a foursome. Eugene Gauss, CEO of Northern Star Minerals, would be Darrell's partner. Our daughter, Debbie, and I would each paddle one of the Monarchs.

In May we contacted Wasa Wasa Adventures at Whitehorse to rent an eighteen-foot tandem canoe for the final three weeks of July. I would drive there with all the camping gear and the two solo canoes atop my Aerostar, unload at Wasa Wasa and proceed on to Fairbanks. Then I would drive the Steese Highway and park the van near Dick and Erla Hutchinson's store in Circle, Alaska. Then Eugene, Darrell and Debbie would fly in and meet me in Fairbanks on July 10. From there the four of us would fly back to Whitehorse to begin the descent of the Yukon River.

On Friday morning, July 2, I began the 4,240-mile drive to the northwest. Whitehorse, capital city of Canada's Yukon Territory, came into view on the following Tuesday. The five-day drive was uneventful except for a day of terrific head winds while crossing Saskatchewan and hitting the brakes in a skid to narrowly miss a woodlands caribou as it crossed the highway in Murdo Lake Provincial Park. While driving across northern Alberta and British Columbia lots of wildlife came into view. There were several moose, lots of mountain sheep, two large black bears as well as an abundant supply of caribou.

On Tuesday evening I unloaded the canoes and camping packs at Wasa Wasa with the assistance of manager Fritz. Then at four the next morning I hit the road for Fairbanks. The gorgeous scenery around Klaune Lake was enjoyable but during the day I encountered the real "Scourge of the North." We used to think mosquitoes and black flies were the "Scourge"—not so! The real "Scourge of the North" if you are on the highway is RVs, motor homes, and campers! Many of them poke along at 25 to 30 miles per hour enjoying the scenery, never thinking of those waiting in line behind.

Alaska—the state I had wanted to see since before it was a state—came into view at mid-day. Then Fairbanks showed up early in the evening. The date was July 7. I had finally made it to Alaska, even though it had taken me more than seventy-four years. Now I would have three days to sample life in central Alaska. On Thursday I drove the 212 miles of the Steese Highway north to Circle, parking the Aerostar to fly back to Fairbanks. On Friday I caught a ride to the University of Alaska, wanting to see the campus and the dairy farm where in 1943 I had an opportunity to become manager of the University's dairy herd. I also wanted to see the muskox herd that, of course, I was interested in since my narrow escape in 1974 along the Thelon River, as described in ***Cold Summer Wind***.

Walking up the hill into the center of the campus, I entered the library and was given a map. The librarian pointed out the muskox farm and the place where the dairy farm buildings were. I failed to ask the distance assuming it was a short way down the hill to the northwest. Following the map, I had walked another four miles to find the muskox herd grazing in a field. Then following the road around the west side of the campus, I found the old dairy farm and house where Mrs. Klein and I would have lived, had we accepted the position offered to us so many years before. Walking on back to my room near the airport, my pedometer showed fourteen miles as the distance walked during the day.

My three canoeing partners arrived on Sunday morning at 4:30. Five hours later we boarded Air North's Queen Air flight to Dawson City and Whitehorse. Prior to departure Air North's Carol Scholl mentioned that one of us might have to be bumped in Dawson. This is precisely what happened. Debbie chose to be the bumpee, while Eugene, Darrell and I continued on to Whitehorse. Therefore, it was late Monday afternoon when we were finally underway down the Yukon, putting in below Whitehorse at the mouth of the Takhini River not far from Wasa Wasa Adventure's base. Two hours later we were setting up camp at the southeast corner of Lake Laberge.

The mountainous scenery was splendid under sunny skies the next day as we moved to the north on Laberge, the lake made famous by Robert W. Service in "The Cremation of Sam McGee." We found a good campsite on the Old Dawson Trail after moving along more than twenty miles. A couple of black bears showed up along the shore just before we selected the place to encamp. Deb's tent was near the food packs. We all hoped she would hear those bears in case they moved in while we were asleep. Eugene built a nice campfire each evening after Darrell served up another of his great dinners.

The next morning we stopped at the old trading post at Lower Laberge as we again entered the river. And what a river! Lots of current with deep and clear water moving on down toward the Bering Sea. We zipped along at more than fifty miles per day with stops at Hootalinque, Big Salmon and Carmacks where Eugene decided to leave us. He needed to be at an important business meeting in Texas early the following week and was concerned that we might not reach Dawson City in time for him to connect with his scheduled flight out. Too bad to see him leave. He was fun to have along.

The famous "Five Fingers Rapids" was our challenge on the following day. Now Darrell paddled the big Old Town Discovery canoe alone. He went on ahead as we approached the rapids to look it over. Soon, he hollered back, "It looks good! Follow me!" This we did and breezed along keeping to the right of the four island group. Then forty-five minutes later we shot down through Rink Rapids. Then came more down river with stops at the abandoned Yukon Cross-

Alaska Pipeline along Steese Highway north of Fairbanks

ing, past Minto to Fort Selkirk, a village that died out when the paddle-wheel boats quit running up and down the river in 1953. On the third day below Five Fingers, while passing the mouth of the White River, came a real surprise. The inflowing water from the west joining the Yukon was actually white, the color of milk. The river was appropriately named. For a couple of miles we paddled near the right riverbank in crystal clear water while the white stuff followed along to our left. Before we rounded the bend above Stewart River the entire Yukon flowed with white silt from the melting glaciers out of the White River. In fact, we were to find no more crystal clear water in our descent of the Yukon.

The usual steep and mountainous Yukon River banks often made finding good campsites nearly impossible. One evening we finally chose a sandy island. By 7:30 the tents were set and Darrell was cooking spaghetti when the first gust of wind hit. Sand began to fly. This was rapidly followed by ever increasingly stronger blasts. Blowing sand and silt filled the air! Debbie's tent was the first to fall! On following gusts mine and then Darrell's tents also went rolling. We quickly secured them with rocks and driftwood poles to keep them on our island as the gale howled on. Finally finding a log, we three sat there with backs to the wind, eyes mostly closed and breathing through handkerchiefs to avoid inhaling the silt for the next two hours, until the velocity of the gusts began to decrease. We re-erected the tents, dumped the cold sand mixed spaghetti, had a quick snack from the lunch bag and crawled into the tents as rain began to pour down. The next morning we tried to clean up the mess. Everything, including tents and sleeping bags, was full up with sand and silt. We named the place "Sand Trap Camp."

Then it was on down river. A day and a half later we arrived in Dawson. We called home from the RV camp and gladly paid one loonie each for a badly needed shower, filled our water jug and were soon back on the river. The mountain scenery was wonderful and wildlife plentiful. Darrell videotaped a grizzly walking along near shore and we enjoyed a close-up look at a cow moose with her calf. High up the mountainsides we often watched the white mountain goats moving around. Two days later we crossed into Alaska.

There were two outstanding occurrences during our final four and a half days on the river. One was seeing the numerous fish-wheels as they turned. Most memorable was the day we made an unexpected stop as a thunderstorm suddenly moved in over the mountains hitting us with a cold, windblasted downpour. Worst of all, as we hit the brush-covered riverbank, the canoes were only partly pulled out of the water and secured. Quickly throwing tarps over them to keep the packs dry, we ran up the steep slope to get under the nearest overhang of a sizeable spruce tree. Then came a thirty-minute downpour followed by a roar from up-river. Here came a convoy of four large high-powered cabin cruisers "going like sixty," only about a hundred feet off shore. We anticipated they would slow down when they sighted our canoes. But, they roared past at full speed, each causing a huge wake to roll right at our loaded boats.

Yes, you guessed it. By the time we rushed down to the canoes, even though they remained upright, most of our packs were floating in the nearly half-filled canoes. Unloading as quickly as possible before too much water seeped into the packs, we did have a few choice words for those people. They never heard what we had to say for, by then, those cruisers were out of sight around the next bend of the river. After pulling the three canoes out of the river and tipping them to drain, we re-loaded and once more headed on down stream.

We arrived in Circle before noon on Monday, July 26 completing the 669 miles of paddling a portion of the Yukon River where no portages were required. The Aerostar was waiting for us. We loaded everything including the canoes on top and headed south to Fairbanks. Darrell flew home. Debbie and I returned the Old Town to Fritz at Wasa Wasa and arrived back in Michigan seven days later.

13

Charged by a Wolverine

After two years of dreaming about the thousands of lakes and numerous rivers in the north country we still wanted to see, in early July of 1995, Darrell and I again headed 'North of 60.' This time we would drive our Ford Aerostar to the end of the road at Points North, Saskatchewan. Then we would fly into Northwest Territories and begin our journey in Vermette Lake. This would put us in the very headwaters of the Elk River, one of the major feeder streams of the Thelon River. We planned to follow the Elk downstream through Rennie and Damant Lake, then turn east through Jarvis, then south and eventually end the journey in Pixley Bay of Selwyn Lake, Saskatchewan. If all went according to plan we would paddle in the headwaters of three of Canada's major rivers. From the Thelon it would be across the height of land into the Dubuant watershed and finally upon entering Selwyn Lake we would be in the waters of the Mackenzie River system.

While at Points North we met Bob Voss who worked as a fly fishing instructor and guide. When he learned of our planned route, he told us many things about the lakes and rivers we would be paddling through. Bob told us of a couple of fishing lodges where he had worked. One was Selwyn Lake Lodge, just a few

Bob Voss, fly fishing instructor

miles south of the 60th parallel. He said we would see it off to our right as we headed for our Pixley Bay pickup. He said, "You fellows should stop there. The lodge owner is Gordon Wallace. Nice guy. I'm sure he'd like to talk with you."

Bob also told us of a place near the Dubuant River in Hinde Lake where he believes the Japanese had a communications base established and ready to operate during World War II.

"It was built in the side of an esker," he said. "The roof had been covered with sand making it invisible from the air, however when I found it the roof was partially caved in. Inside of the place I found more than a thousand dry cell batteries and they all had Japanese printing on them."

"How long ago did you find the place?" I asked.

"Let's see now. Guess it has been about fourteen or fifteen years. It was back in a bay along the west side of the lake. Hinde will not be along your route of travel but as you fellows make the crossing between Flett and Selwyn Lakes you will be only a short distance from the Chipewyan Indians' 'Sacred Lake.'" Then Mr. Voss continued telling many fascinating stories about Sacred Lake. One was of a time when he helped to carry a crippled woman on a stretcher into Sacred Lake. They dipped her into the lake of the Great Spirit and in a few minutes she got up and walked with them back to their boat at Selwyn Lake. Little did we know then how our chat with Bob Voss would affect our travels in the north during the next five years.

We wondered: Could this be Mr. Jonsson's base camp?

Debbie Klein looks under the missing corner of a huge rock.

Ragnar Jonsson in 1983

Ragnar and the Author at Nueltin Lake

The Thlewiaza River flows into Nueltin Lake

We climb out of Artillery Lake to cross Pike's Portage.

Solid ice blocks our route to Windy River Post in July of 2000

Ragnar's monument in 2001

Monument Point from esker on Jonsson Island

Darrell Klein relaxes against a huge spruce—Poor Fish River

Clayton Klein on the final portage along Windy River

Schweder's old cook stove at Windy River Post

PHOTO COURTESY OF GORDON WALLACE

Sacred Lake (Gootway) of the Chipewyans

Sacred Lake from the air looking over Sacred Mountain

A thunderstorm moves toward our Flett Lake camp

Our campsite on Lucy Island in Selwyn Lake

It was the morning of July 11 before a Points North Beaver was available to fly us the 214 miles with our two Mad River Monarch canoes to a beach at the south end of Vermette Lake. The plane was equipped with a GPS and I was amazed at its accuracy. What a miracle!

Within a half-hour the canoes were loaded and we pushed away from shore. Our route for the first couple of days took us mainly north across Vermette and Rennie Lakes. Both of these days we faced and at times forced our way directly into a strong north wind. On an esker along the east side of Rennie we stretched our legs as we visited a trapper's cabin. There was no one home. Apparently the owner had gone outside for the summer.

Three miles east of our campsite the next morning, we entered the Elk River proper. It was all downhill for the next forty-five minutes as we descended the thirteen feet into Damant Lake without making a portage. With a strong wind blowing we bounced over the waves passing our 'Sick Beach' where we started our Thelon River journey in 1974. Soon we entered Jarvis Lake and camped in the evening on an esker along the left. Walking a couple of miles in the bright sunshine the esker was indeed beautiful! We watched as a family of arctic fox frolicked along a nearby slope. Birds were everywhere. Arctic terns chattered constantly and in the distance we could hear the calls of sandhill cranes and red-throated loons.

A three-hour paddle the next morning took us to the southeast corner of Jarvis Lake. Our zigzag route from there on would be mainly south for the next two hundred miles across the 60th parallel into Saskatchewan. Now it was portage time. First came a short one into a small lake followed by a full mile carry into a large unnamed lake. By the time we had completed these portages we had walked at least seven miles under full load. When we arrived at the south end of the second lake it was 4:00 P.M. We had had enough and pitched our tents on a nearby esker. After supper we walked down to Lake 1256 and learned we would have only a quarter mile carry next morning.

Our travels to this point were mainly along the edge of the Barrens, with occasional small clumps of black spruce and low brush. The portages were simple carries between lakes with no specific trail to follow. The going was fairly easy except for crossing rocky ravines and muskeg flats. Soon we would be entering taiga country with small trees most everywhere.

With good weather and no wind the black flies, mosquitoes and other insects gave us a bad time in camp and on the portages. This was definitely headnet time. While we were cooking, they constantly fell into the hot pots, pans, and cups. We learned to eat with headnets on. This is done by quickly lifting the net to a position just above your mouth with one hand as you pop a spoon or fork full of food in, then instantly dropping the net as you chew and prepare for the next spoonful. It is impossible to eat a meal without also consuming dozens of those little critters. If you pause to pick one or two out of your cup or off the plate, dozens more will fall in as you do so. Thus you eat scores of them as you enjoy camping north of 60 in mid July.

Four portages on July 15 under cloudy skies and we had entered Firedrake Lake. Paddling south the rain came down most of the afternoon. We encamped above a little beach along the east shore. Between showers as I rounded up some fuel for a fire, Darrell paddled out a short distance with a fishing rod and soon returned with two nice lake trout. They made us a delicious supper with plenty left over for breakfast.

The rains continued until mid-forenoon next day. We paddled along under cloudy skies and a breeze out of the northeast. During the afternoon, while moving along near the west shore of Firedrake, Darrell saw something moving on the rocky shore ahead. On such a dark and cloudy day we were unable to immediately identify the object. At first we thought it was a grizzly. But no! Drawing closer we could hear growls and snarls. There were two large dark brown animals. They were fighting. They were wolverines.

Darrell quickly picked up his video camera ready to shoot some footage as we moved closer. The animals continued their snarling battle until we were less than forty feet away. Then the excitement began. The wolverines saw us! Instantly one of them jumped off the rocky ledge with a splash and began swimming full speed for Darrell's canoe. I was only a paddle length to the side. Instinctively I gripped my paddle to help fight off the beast. When only eight to ten feet short of the canoe, the wolverine suddenly stopped, turned and rapidly swam back toward shore, jumping up on the rocky ledge beside the other animal who had been keeping an eye on the entire scene. Together both of them quickly disappeared behind the nearby ridge of huge boulders.

While the swimming wolverine headed back for shore, I suddenly woke up and grabbed my trusty camera. By the time it was focused and ready to shoot, the animals were disappearing between the boulders. What a disappointment! In all of our previous travels we had seen only a single wolverine on two occasions. Now, I had sat there spellbound in sort of a daze during this action. I couldn't believe what was happening and didn't get a single photo. "That's a sure sign of old age," I quipped as we discussed the situation and paddled on to the south.

Later in the afternoon we were 'blown off' the lake by gale force winds but moved on in the evening nearly to the south end of Firedrake. Seven portages during the next couple of days took us across Jost, Viera and four smaller unnamed lakes, and we were crossing Anaunethad Lake. Then came the rain. Lots of it for several hours caused us to miss our supper but the sleeping was as good

Darrell preps supper in the Flett to Selwyn Trail

as it always is in a tent when snuggled in a goosedown bag. Leaving Anaunethad it was down the Dubuant River and around a bend to the left for a half-mile and we had entered Wholdaia Lake. Then it was more flat-water paddling for a couple of days as strong northeast winds and frequent rains persisted.

On July 21 we crossed the portage trail into the north end of Flett Lake. The old trail was as difficult as I remembered it to be from when daughter Debbie and I had crossed it back in 1981.

Darrell and I had taken only about three hundred paddle stokes on Flett when a sudden thunderstorm formed up with a 'bang' directly overhead. At full speed we headed for shore but were caught in a sheet of falling water. Wet to the skin, in a few minutes we were again underway as the sun popped out.

Frequent rains and strong winds persisted and it required another two days to move to the south end of Flett Lake. Arriving there, we searched for nearly an hour before finding the portage trail leading up and over the hills to Selwyn Lake. From our maps we knew the length of this trail was nearly two miles. It was late in the day so we decided to camp somewhere along the trail. Underway with our first load of gear at 5:30 we found a place to set up the tents after stepping along for more than a mile. Then back we went to bring up another load. This time Darrell also carried along Baggies of water from Flett for campsite cooking. While eating supper I remarked, "That mountain over there must be the Chipewyan's Sacred Mountain. The one Bob Voss told us about."

"Yep. That must be the one with a hole in the top overlooking the Sacred Lake. Wish we had time to check it out in the morning but there's not time. We better keep moving as fast as we can. We have only a couple of days to get down into Pixley Bay to meet the Points North flight for our pre-scheduled pickup and most likely the wind will stop us somewhere along the way."

Early the next morning we completed the nearly two mile portage and were paddling south on Selwyn Lake by 10:00. The wind was strong from the northwest. Then came more rain. We island hopped to avoid as much of the heavy seas as possible. By mid-afternoon as gale force winds whipped up, we were again blown off the lake putting ashore on some big rocks at the tip of an island. With no letup in the wind velocity during the evening we were forced to overnight nearby. This delay caused us considerable worry. We would have to make the final twenty-six miles on the following day. Before retiring, once again we used the Indian alarm clock technique of drinking the correct amount of water before we turned in. From past experiences we had each learned the exact amount to drink when we wanted to sleep only six hours. We both set our built in alarm clocks for 4:30 the next morning. Mine, however, being nearly worn out, went off at 4:20. Darrell soon had a fire blazing and following a quick breakfast we broke camp and were stroking the water at 5:30.

The going was good. It was a nice morning with a breeze from the north. Six hours later we were back in northern Saskatchewan. Somewhat later, looking to the southwest, we could see Selwyn Lake Lodge. We decided to go over and ask them to contact Points North for us, letting them know we were on schedule and

Mary, Nigel, Becky and Gordon Wallace: Selwyn Lake Lodge

would be ready for pickup in Pixley Bay the next morning. Arriving at the Lodge on Common Island we soon met Gordon Wallace. He asked where we came from as canoes seldom travel through the area. When he learned we had started in the Elk River, he wanted to talk about our travels and asked us to stay overnight at the Lodge as his guests. He showed us to our room and while we had hot showers, called Points North. Shortly he returned with good news. Points North would pick us up at the Lodge dock next morning.

We chatted for a few minutes about things to the north. Gordon was busy. He soon departed to fly a couple of guests to Stony Rapids but was back in time for dinner. As the fishing boats returned we were surprised to again meet Bob Voss who was serving as a guide for a few days. When Gordon returned he introduced us to his wife Mary, daughter Becky and son Nigel who were helping with work at the Lodge. At dinner we met the other guests including Chris Helms and his son from Toledo, Ohio. The dinner was scrumptious; better than anything normally found in the finest of gourmet restaurants. We soon learned that Selwyn Lake Lodge is an angler's paradise. While the guests chatted about their fishing exploits, Gordon kept asking about our trips down the Cochrane, Kazan and Thelon Rivers, he enthusiastically remarked, "You should write a book about your trips."

"I already have," I replied.

"Wonderful! How can I get a copy and what's the title?"

"***Cold Summer Wind*** and I'll send you a copy as soon as we get back to Michigan."

Darrell and I asked various questions about the Lodge and the area. Soon Gordon asked if we had been to the Sacred Lake of the Chipewyan's. Giving him a negative reply, he went on to say, "You were close to it when you came across the trail from Flett Lake. It is at the base of the mountain, east of the trail. Many of the people still believe their Great Spirit lives up there in Sacred Lake and the mountain overlooking the lake."

"I wish we had known where to find it. We'd like to know more about it. When Bob Voss was telling us about it, at Points North, he was saying the Lake seldom freezes over in the wintertime. Is that really true?"

"Well, almost. The water stays open there until all the other lakes around here are deeply frozen. You should talk with guides Billy Joe and Pierre. They could tell you all about it. Pierre was born over on the east shore of Selwyn and has spent most of his life in this area."

Later Gordon introduced us to Billy Joe Mercredi, whose father was also born nearby, and to Pierre Broussie, telling them we were interested in information about Sacred Lake. We chatted while Gordon talked with other guests. We soon learned that old Pierre didn't speak our language, however, he appeared to understand most everything we said. Billy Joe tried to be helpful and did answer a few questions. It soon became apparent, Pierre didn't want us to learn too much. They often spoke to each other in Chipewyan and to some questions we noticed Pierre would shake his head when Billy Joe was looking his way.

The next morning Billy Joe spoke briefly with me and did confirm that Sacred Lake really does not solidly freeze over in the wintertime and the water continually moves around and around in the lake. With his arm he motioned in a counter clockwise circle as he spoke.

Following a big breakfast we attempted to settle up with Gordon to cover some of his costs. He would accept no payment. "It was a pleasure to have you here," he said. "I've learned so much from you. Just send me a copy of ***Cold Summer Wind***."

14

Solo to Selwyn

Before 1996 began I had decided to learn more about Sacred Lake. I would need facts and photos before I could write about it. 'Curiosity killed the cat,' according to the old cliché. Personal observation was needed to satisfy this curiosity. This time I would be on my own and traveling alone. My camping partner Darrell was not able to get away from his duties as General Manager of the family fertilizer business. On Friday morning, July 12, with loaded van and canoe on top I headed for Points North Air Base in northern Saskatchewan.

Three days later in mid-afternoon I was flown 225 miles north by pilot Lyle Urich in a Cessna 185. He put me down on an island in northern Firedrake Lake. This is where another of my life's adventures began. Now the question was, could I find my way back to civilization? I was confident I could. Darrell had assured the folks at home that indeed I could, but some still had their doubts.

Rain showers with a few brief sunny periods were frequent during the first couple of days as I moved south on Firedrake and across Jost Lake. There were no real portage trails between the small lakes south of Jost so the going was far from easy. The second carry was through a rocky swamp and up and over an esker. The black flies were horrific along the way. I lunched and relaxed in the canoe while crossing the little lakes enroute.

While crossing those lakes there was plenty of time to enjoy the solitude and think about my good fortune of being able to get away from the rat race of civilization on occasions like this. Whether paddling through the wilderness alone or with friends or family, it's indeed wonderful to move along for days or weeks without seeing any other people. Places where rivers, lakes and ancient trails are the only highways. Where neither railroads nor bridges exist within hundreds of miles. Most people nowadays are unable to experience this feeling of enjoyment and quiet solitude even once in their entire lifetimes.

These feelings have, on many occasions, almost overwhelmed me. They were best put into words many years ago by the late Siguard F. Olson and published in his book ***The Lonely Land***. From my recollections, I think it went something like this:

> "The movement of a canoe is like a reed in the wind. Silence is a part of it, and the sounds of lapping water, bird songs and wind in the trees. A canoe is a part of the medium through which it floats, the sky, the water and the shores. A man is part of his canoe and therefore, part of all it knows. The instant he dips his paddle, he flows as it flows, the canoe yielding to his slightest touch and responsive to his every thought and whim...There is a magic in the feel of a paddle and the movement of a canoe, a magic compounded by distance, adventure, a feeling of a nearness to God, solitude and peace. The way of the canoe is the way of the wilderness and of a freedom almost forgotten. It's the open door to waterways of ages past and a way of life with profound and abiding satisfactions."

July 18 was a day to remember. The weather was good while crossing Viera Lake. It was two hours on the paddle followed by a carry over into Lakes 1227 and 1226. Then moving east and south for a couple of hours, I came to an almost impossible portage, so it seemed. Finding the start of a trail I lost it while crossing the higher ground. Finally a trail showed up again down near the small lake I sought. On the return trip I again lost the trail on the high ground. The exact same happened on my second carry and return making progress slow. By this time I should have learned the way across. Finally I shouldered the canoe but lost the trail four times and each time had to turn it around in the small trees and bushes and get back to the trail.

Tired and after 6 P.M. with no place there to camp I did a 'No! No!' I loaded the canoe heading down into the previously unnamed lake bow first. Shoving it into the water as far as possible without getting water in my boots, I climbed in. That was another mistake for the stern was still stuck on shore. Pushing on the

I had paddled more than a mile east of the trail-head

paddle we moved a little. Then another push and the canoe broke free of the shore and tipped to the right. I fell in the lake. Wading back on shore, I hauled the canoe up and unloaded everything. There were six to eight inches of water to be dumped before reloading. The black flies were unmerciful, as I moved the canoe out stern first and shoved away from shore. By this time the sky was socked in with cold, gray clouds.

Paddling south on the nearly two mile long lake, I needed a campsite as soon as possible. I needed to get ashore and let things dry out. Good campsites were few and far between. I soon arrived at the end of the lake and could see a trail leading up to higher ground. Now the problem was, just how to get up on shore as large rocks extended out into the water for about thirty feet. The tops of most of them were near the lake's surface, some just below and some a foot or two above the water. Without hesitation I carefully stepped out on a rock with rope in hand and pulled the canoe. A foot slipped and unfortunately I fell into the lake again. Climbing out I cautiously stepped from rock to rock toward shore. Giving the rope another pull, once more I lost my balance and this time fortunately fell into a deep spot between rocks where even my face went underwater. By then my face certainly needed washing anyway. Finally ashore I dug dry clothes from my pack and removed the wet as the insects bored in. Pouring the water out of my boots, dry things went on, right there on the trail. It would have made a good photo. While the tent was going up that evening, this small and previously unnamed lake had earned its name. It is now known as 'Fall-In Lake.'

The next morning as the wet things dried in a strong south wind, I carried the canoe along a good trail to the north end of Anaunethad Lake. By mid-forenoon I was paddling but making little progress in the face of the wind on this large lake. Four hours of fun, struggling and bouncing over the waves was enough and I sought shelter along the east shore.

During the following two days I crossed both Anaunethad and Wholdaia Lakes and portaged across into Flett Lake by late afternoon. It was raining, and needing a campsite, I headed south along the east shore. Strong northwest winds and waves breaking over the rocks along shore made any landing impossible. It was seven in the evening before I rounded a point halfway down the lake and encamped. Rain fell all night and until nearly noon. Once underway the sky soon cleared. Passing several islands, the rugged hills become higher and higher as one approaches the southern end of Flett. Camping that night on the little peninsula where Debbie and I had camped in 1981, I was surprised to find an abandoned trapper's cabin in the identical place.

Flett Lake's east shore where rain fell all nght

On Tuesday morning, July 28, I made the long portage over into Selwyn Lake in five hours. My plan was to set up camp east of the trailhead, then take a full day, if necessary, to find, photograph and explore around Sacred Lake. Little did I know while crossing the portage, just how close I was to the Holy Lake of the Chipewyans. Sacred Lake is so small it does not show on the 1: 250,000-scale map I was using. I had paddled more than a mile east of the trailhead before finding a satisfactory camping place. It was a weather perfect day with loons whooping it up nearby. I did some laundry and went for a swim, getting a much-needed bath.

Wednesday morning dawned cloudy and windless. Right after breakfast, with headnet on, lunch, map, and camera packed and compass in hand I headed up some very steep hills. Climbing north and west through thick brush, over and around huge rocks I finally gained the summit. Soon my compass indicated I was plenty far west so walking more to the north, down across a valley and over a second crest, I could see a small lake to the east. Following the north slope of the ridge, I soon came out above a sheer cliff with the little lake about two hundred feet directly below. There was no easy way down so I sat on the ledge enjoying the view while taking photos of the scene.

Clear blue sky reappeared as I returned to camp by mid-day. With a light breeze from the north I decided to pack up and head south toward Saskatchewan. The going was good as I crossed the bay. I heard thunder in the southwest even though the sun was shining. Five minutes later there was a strange roaring sound to the north, behind me. Looking around, a gale was whipping up across the bay bearing down on me. It soon caught me as I rushed for the nearest island. If I could make it to the downwind side of the island I might get ashore. Bouncing broadside to the wind and up and over each wave with water splashing and blowing across the canoe, I made the lee shore of the island. Soon a dense fog moved in. A cold front was moving through and the wind howled on. I soon discovered a level spot big enough for the tent and camped over on the little island.

With twenty-five miles of Selwyn Lake to cover to make it to the Lodge on Common Island I was stroking the water by five o'clock the next morning. A breeze from the northeast assisted and I crossed the 60th parallel at noon, arriving at the Lodge a couple of hours later. Walking up and into the dining room, I was met by Mary Wallace; she and Gordon were soon giving me the Selwyn Lake Lodge welcome. He assigned me a room and asked if I had found Sacred Lake. Assuring him affirmatively, I soon showered, put on clean clothes and relaxed.

At my request Gordon contacted Points North for my pickup next morning. He asked where I had paddled from. Then as the guests of the Lodge and guides returned from their day of fishing I was soon introduced to everyone as the author who had just paddled 175 miles to have dinner with them.

Following a scrumptious and elegantly served dinner, Gordon introduced me to guide John Louis Youya of Stoney Rapids, Saskatchewan. Youya's uncle William owned the cabins we had found at Obre Lake in 1968 and had written of

John Louis Youya

in ***Cold Summer Wind***. As we chatted I asked John Louis if he had ever been to Obre Lake?

"Yes. I helped Uncle Bill on his trapline the winter I was fourteen years old."

Gordon then cut in, "Mr. Klein would like to know more about your Holy Lake. He was up there yesterday so tell him anything you can about it."

"Well," he hesitated, looking around. "Our elders don't like us to talk about it much to outsiders. But I can tell you a little. Last year my mother had a very sore face. Some bad kind of rash. An infection. The nursing station in Stony was unable to give her anything that helped. The rash lasted for months. In December I went by Skidoo to Sacred Lake, cut out a block of ice and took it back to her. We melted it down. She bathed her face in that water several times and in a few days she was OK again."

"Very interesting," I replied. "The water from the lake must have healing powers."

"It does! It does! And HE lives up there in the lake and mountain." All was quiet for a minute. Then John Louis told about the many sick people who have been cured from all kinds of diseases after drinking or bathing in the lake's water. "There was a lady from Black Lake," he continued, "who couldn't walk. We took her to the lake on a stretcher. She bathed in the water for two days. She got up on her feet and is walking again. The leaves on the plants close around the lake stay green all winter," he continued. "There is one kind of plant up there that looks and tastes like celery. Did you notice it while you were there?"

"No! I was unable to get down close to the lake. I sat on that high ledge south of the lake and looked down at it."

A puzzled look came over John Louis' face. Shaking his head he paused, then asked, "Do you have a map?"

"Yes. It's in my room."

"Let's look at it. Can you get it?"

"Sure. Be back in a minute."

When I returned with a map of the area, focusing his eyes on it, John Louis said, "Now show me just where you were."

With pen in hand, I pointed to the place I had camped and showed him my route up and over the high hills to the little lake. Glancing at his face I noticed he was grinning and shaking his head from side to side saying "Nooo! You were at wrong lake. Sacred Lake is over here," he pointed. "Just below big mountain and not far off the road from Flett to Selwyn. When you came across from Flett, did you see big rock close to the road?"

I was shocked, amazed and bewildered at his announcement. Disappointedly replying, "Probably did. Seems like there were several big rocks along there."

"There is one huge rock. If you go east from the rock you'll find trail going

Sacred Mountain across the lake

down to lake. You'll see big mountain across the lake. It's our Sacred Mountain."

The announcement had taken the wind out of my sails. In despair after thanking him for the information, I soon departed for my room wondering what to do. I had taken photos of the wrong lake! The next morning with the Points North plane due within the hour, at breakfast Gordon chatted with me. He said, "Mary has been wanting to see Sacred Lake for a long time. When our season slows down she and I'll go up there for a look around. I'll take my camera and get some pictures for you."

"That would be appreciated. I really would like a photo of the lake." Soon the Cessna 185 from Points North splashed down, taxied to the dock and shortly I was on my way back to Michigan.

15

Sacred Lake

When 1997 rolled in, Darrell and I were making plans for another summer journey into the North. This time we would start in Bradford Lake right on the 60th parallel and descend the stream flowing north into the Kazan River. Then it would be upstream on the Kazan into Snowbird Lake and northwest over the height of land into the eastern branch of the upper Dubuant River. We would follow that stream down across the 61st parallel where we wanted to check out the old Japanese Communications setup that Bob Voss had told us about. From there we would turn to the southwest and again wrap up the journey at Selwyn Lake Lodge.

While growing up on the farm where I still live near Fowlerville, Michigan, my parents were some of my best instructors. When any project failed to succeed as planned, my dad would say, "If you don't at first succeed, try-try again." Those words of advice have remained with me and became a part of my life. So, now I would have another opportunity to try to find Sacred Lake. I still wanted to visit the place even though Gordon Wallace had sent some good photos the previous autumn.

Over the years we have learned that most of the biting insects have disappeared by mid-July along the 60th so it was July 17 when Lyle Urich flew the two of us into Bradford Lake. It was headnet time as soon as we could get them out of our packs. We were wearing them before Lyle and the Otter had cleared the lake. The insects were merciless those first few days.

The next morning, heading downstream, we shot two sets of rapids before making a short-cut portage to the west over into the Kazan River. From there it was upstream paddling for the next fifty-five miles. Soon we came upon one of the Kazan's major unmarked rapids. There were several other drops in the river to carry around as well. Paddling with power was often required at times to gain a foot or two per stroke in the fast flowing river. There were times when Darrell, with his skill and strength, could push on up a riffle, but his dad lacked the power to make it up the same grade. I would then maneuver over near shore and rope my canoe up to where Darrell either waited or came back to help. I recalled a conversation with Verlen Kruger when I once asked him how he managed to paddle upstream on the fast flowing Yukon River. "Paddling upstream is no more difficult than paddling down," he replied with a grin. "The only difference is, you just don't make as many miles per day."

Upstream on the Kazan was enjoyable, though not easy. Three days were required to move up through Atzinging and Obre Lakes. We passed Obre Lake Lodge without stopping as heavy roaring equipment extending the landing strip of the Lodge kicked up a terrific cloud of dust. A good trail leading past the rapids below Snowbird Lake made the going there fairly easy. Once past Snowbird Lodge we sought a campsite and found a place on the north side of the peninsula.

Nine hours of paddling under a clear blue, sunny sky took us twenty-two miles to the northwest shore of Snowbird. We camped above a pebble beach on the island where we had camped in July of 1968 while traveling with nephews Brian Beasley and Loren Jonckheere while enroute to Reindeer Lake. "We were twenty-nine years younger than we are now," Darrell remarked as he prepared our spaghetti dinner.

"That's for sure. After today's paddle in the 85-degree sunshine, I really feel like I'm twenty-nine years older, and those were twenty-nine good years, too!"

The next morning, July 23, dawned bright and clear. Another perfect day. We paddled on north about six miles into the bay east of Lake One. Our plan was to portage and paddle, crossing four smaller lakes along the tree line and over the height of land to the west into a stream flowing into Dubuant River. Glancing at our maps made the crossing look easy.

Spirits were high as with backpacks on and smaller packs in each hand we headed through the bushes and small trees up the hill to the west. Once up the slope and out of the trees we found ourselves on a fairly level plateau with lots of water and muskeg to work our way around or through to get to the lake we called

Lake One. It was a rough go with no trail to follow and it was definitely headnet time as hoards of insects continually bored down on us in the 80-degree plus temperature, but we eventually made it.

Returning to Snowbird we each shouldered a canoe for the second crossing. On the third trip up the hill we carried the remaining pieces of gear. By four in the afternoon we were paddling across Lake One through flocks of ducks, geese, and many varieties of shore birds. In camp during the evening, Darrell turned on his new GPS and found our position to be 60.49 North Latitude and 102.53 West Longitude.

A heavy thunderstorm moved in during the night with lightning strikes too close for comfort. The rain continued and it was mid-day before we were able to get underway across the sub-arctic tundra. Our struggle across the water-laced wilderness continued while finding and crossing Lakes Two and Three. The rains returned as we encamped that evening.

With more than an additional mile of carry to get to Lake Four, we started out when the rain let up early the next morning. In our bogged-down condition and with no trails to follow, we were no longer shouldering the canoes as we always had. Now we were dragging them behind with the bow rope looped around our waists. This portage looked fairly easy at the start but then came a marshy, brushy bog with gnarled willows and thick tag elders extending in all directions above our heads. With backpacks on and heavily loaded we entered the area thinking

We enter Lake #3

Our final look at Lake #3

we would soon be on solid ground again. To our surprise while walking through, trying to step around the thick elders and from bog to bog, we came upon a creek. It had to be crossed. There was no dry place to set down the heavy packs. We moved ahead, wading the creek's waist-deep water. We were unprepared for the creek, as it was not shown on our maps. A couple of hundred yards beyond we came to higher ground where we dropped our packs to return through the creek and pull the canoes and other gear along. This time we crossed the creek in the Monarchs, dumped water out of our boots, put on dry socks and continued to the west.

Late in the afternoon we arrived at Lake Four. Now we were across the height of land. Soon we would be moving down toward the Dubuant River.

A couple of days later, while camping on an island in Sherwood Lake, we again studied our maps and time and distance schedule. According to the trip plan we were then three full days behind schedule. Darrell needed to be back at work ten days later. Time and my energy were both running out, mainly time. Thus we decided to bypass the Hinde Lake portion of the journey. Now we would follow the unnamed creek ahead, which we called the east branch of the upper Dubuant River, down into Wholdaia Lake. Then we would move up into Flett Lake and use the time gained to explore around Sacred Lake.

The weather remained good as we moved on down the meandering stream. In this stretch we found more than a half dozen sets of shootable rapids, plus four places requiring portages. Best of all, the lower carries had trails to follow.

On Wednesday, July 29, facing a strong wind from the southwest, we took our lunch break on the little island where the waters of Flett Lake pour down to meet Wholdaia. In mid-afternoon a thunderstorm moved in. We sought shelter on a beach along the west shore and later decided to camp nearby. The next morning it was a four-hour paddle across Flett to the peninsula near the south end where we again encamped. By noon, with cameras and compass in hand, we moved up the Selwyn Lake trail to the big rock, then down in the valley to the east. Finally we had arrived at the Sacred Lake of the Chipewyan's. What a thrill! Standing near the edge of the lake, looking across and up at Sacred Mountain.

We found the celery-like plants growing near the shore and a gallon glass jar turned upside down over the top of a small tree. There is a place at the south end of The Lake where people could bathe in the lake's sacred waters (We later learned the Chipewyan's name for the lake is 'Gootway').

With headnets on we climbed up the mountainside to the east as black flies crawled over us by the thousands. Our intentions were to find the hole in the top of Sacred Mountain, which Bob Voss and others had told us about, but the insect hoard soon turned us back. Big, juicy, ripe cloudberries were plentiful, growing out of the sphagnum on the mountain slope. We could have easily eaten our fill of them but it was a risky business, trying to lift the headnet to pop a couple of berries into our mouths without black flies swarming in at the same time.

Darrell checks the GPS at Sacred Lake

Abandoned cabin—Old village—Selwyn Lake's east shore

Back in camp late in the afternoon we relaxed and enjoyed one of Darrell's delicious dinners. A discussion began when I remarked, "I sure like it around here. The scenery is so good and today we finally found the real Sacred Lake."

"Yes. There must be an underground aqueduct flowing out of Selwyn, down through Sacred and on down into Flett."

"Certainly has to be. Selwyn Lake is at 1,292 feet above sea level and Flett is 1,195. That's a difference of 97 feet in less than two miles. All of that water pouring down out of Selwyn must keep Sacred from freezing over until late in the year."

"And," Darrell added, "The fast flowing water keeps Sacred's water moving around and 'round. That accounts for what we've heard about the plants near shore remaining green throughout the winter. Now it's easy to understand how this situation would have mystified the people who lived around here many centuries ago. Most likely they didn't realize that Selwyn was nearly a hundred feet higher than Flett and, of course, they would have known nothing about an underground aqueduct back in those days."

We were up and at 'em the next morning at 4:30. Six hours later we had completed the three-kilometer trail and were loading the canoes at Selwyn Lake.

Ten miles along the east shore are the remains of an abandoned Chipewyan village. We decided to paddle over into the mile deep bay and find it. Upon arriving we promptly decided to camp over, as the place looked intriguing. Best of all was the scarcity of insects. The place has a creek flowing through a gap in an esker just below a rapid with a little island in the mouth of the creek. Nearby are three vacant cabins still standing.

The day was warm and sunny. When the tents were pitched we roamed the area, enjoying a couple of hours of exploration around the old village. We were amazed at the number of places where cabins had once stood. Certainly hundreds of people had lived there during recent centuries. We later learned this village was once the home of Chipewyan Chief Morris Peche who had signed Treaty 6 with Canada in 1906. He is buried nearby. It is also the birthplace of Pierre Broussie, chief guide at Selwyn Lake Lodge.

Back to our camp, sitting around before supper, we were discussing our struggles since Bradford Lake. Following a pause, Darrell surprised me by saying, "I've been amazed at your energy and the way you move along. You've kept going in rough places where a lot of twenty-five year olds would be unable to carry on." Then he added, "I think you are just about the best dad in the world."

Wow! That shocked me. I knew we were good friends but we had never spoken to each other in such glowing terms. An arctic tern came chattering by as I responded, "Those are mighty kind words. You're a mighty good camping partner, too. I'm fortunate to have a son like you. We've been through a lot together."

"Sure have. The worst of all for me were times on the Back River in North Star II, without a spray cover. I was certainly happy to get away from there alive."

"My biggest scare was when the bull muskox charged me," I replied.

"Mine was the time we were hung up on an unseen rock just above those rapids in the Back River as the fast flowing water turned the canoe end for end and we hung there. Then you finally were able to work us loose from the rock and we shot the rapids stern first."

"I remember it well."

On August 1, in the afternoon, we were once more welcomed to Selwyn Lake Lodge by Gordon Wallace and his family. Following hot showers and a little rest, Gordon took the two of us for a boat ride to visit another old village to the west and north of Common Island. This too had been a sizable settlement in the past. During the evening, after another wonderful gourmet dinner, we chatted again with John Louis Youya about Sacred Lake. Then headed for home the next day.

Gordon Wallace takes us to another Chipewyan Village

16

The Great Spirit

In July of 1998, with the Japanese Communications setup still intriguing us, we headed north again. This time we would definitely go down to Hinde Lake and find it, get some photos and bring back a few of the items they had left behind. We carried along a magnetometer and small shovel to pinpoint and retrieve some of the items.

Starting high up in the west branch of the Dubuant River in Smalltree Lake, we headed downstream. Forest fires were raging all around us. To make a long story short, ten days later while descending a couple of rapids in the northeast end of Wholdaia Lake, we were astounded at the amount of water pouring down. Paddling down those twenty miles where the river drops about eighty feet would be a fun ride but I feared I might not be able to paddle back up again. Darrell had previously learned the "North of 60 Camps" have a fishing lodge on a nearby island. Discussing the volume and speed of the river ahead we decided to find the lodge and ask if one of their planes could come and pick us up at Hinde Lake about a week later.

We soon located the Lodge. The men there, Ned and Dan, did call headquarters at Obre Lake. Speaking with Clark Jennie, the owner and manager of "North of 60 Camps," we soon learned they could not promise to pick us up at Hinde.

Their planes were too far behind schedule. Two of their guides were down. One was burned in the fires raging in the area and the other was out for his wife's funeral who had burned to death in a fire. Furthermore, their cook at the Wholdaia South Lodge had just had a heart attack that very morning.

What a disappointment! In despair, we soon pointed the bow of our canoes back to the south. Four days later we were once more paddling south on Selwyn Lake. High winds forced us ashore on an island with a sand beach only a couple of miles north of the 60th parallel.

Then late on the following day we again paddled up to the dock of Selwyn Lake Lodge and received the usual cordial welcome. The place was full of guests. This time we stayed over in the guide's tent. In the evening, while Darrell chatted with Gordon, I had a good visit with Leon Cook, former Chief of the Black Lake Band of Chipewyans. Pierre Broussie mainly listened with an occasional comment in the native tongue. Knowing we had arrived from Northwest Territories, Chief Leon Cook asked where we had been. I told him about our route from Smalltree to Wholdaia, then back through Flett.

"Did you get near any of those fires?" he asked.

"Yes. The whole country up there seems to be burning over. We had to make one portage of more than a mile through an area that burned over only a day or two before. The fire was still burning a short distance from us."

The two chuckled as Leon asked, "Did you get a little black?"

"Everything became covered with soot, our clothing, packs and even the canoes! The fire has made the country a black wasteland! Such a mess!"

"Where did you stay last night?"

"On an island about two miles north of the Parkhurst Peninsula. The one with the big sandy beach along its south side."

"Lucy!" Pierre exclaimed

Nodding, Leon added, "We call it Lucy Island as that's where Pierre's grandmother Lucy is buried." Then he asked, "Did you see Gootway Lake?"

"No. Not this time. We came through here a year ago and did go down to it then."

Shaking his head with a frown, Leon replied, "HE does not like outsiders visiting HIS Lake or HIS Mountain. Did you take pictures, too?"

"Yes, a few," I responded. Then being uncertain of his reason for these questions, I asked, "What do you call your Great Spirit?" He looked puzzled with no reply, so I added, "We Christians call our Great Spirit 'God,' so I'm wondering if you have a name for the Great Spirit of the Chipewyans?"

"God, yes. I know about him. I learned about God while in school in Stony Rapids. The Anglicans and Catholics have their God. We have our Great Spirit, too, and I know HE lives. HE lives in Sacred Mountain and Sacred Lake."

"Yes. What is your name for him?"

"HE is up there, I know! And HE does not like anyone who is not one of his people walking or looking around up there. When HE gets angry, there will be big troubles. HE sometimes even gets angry when outsiders use the road from Flett to Selwyn. That is HIS area. There are many times when HE has really helped us but HE does get angry, too. I know HE lives and I hope HE has not been made angry because you've been to HIS home!"

Our discussions continued for nearly an hour but Chief Leon did not reveal a name for his Great Spirit, always referring to HE or HIM.

The next morning following breakfast, most of the guests with guides were off to catch the big ones. Gordon went out with Dick Sternburg to do underwater photography of lake trout about seventy feet below the surface for a PBS video. The Points North Otter soon arrived and Darrell and I headed for home.

Andy Eckel, General Manager of Points North Air Base

17

Hinde Lake

During the next several months, the vision of what we might have found had we made it down to Hinde Lake kept turning over in my mind. I just couldn't forget about it. After all, I was planing to write another book and this story could be an important part of it. I didn't know enough about it and just couldn't let a sleeping dog lie. Before Christmas I had again talked Darrell into accompanying me. We would make one final attempt to find the ruins of the Japanese communications setup at Hinde Lake.

On July 11, 1999, we headed north again. This time we would solve the mystery that had haunted our minds ever since Bob Voss had first told us about it five years earlier. We were flown directly to Flett Lake by Andy Eckel, General Manager of Points North Air Base, in one of his Beavers. This time we would paddle our Monarch canoes directly down to Hinde Lake.

Four days later we shot those two sets of rapids and stopped again at 'North of 60s, Wholdaia North Fly-in Lodge' to let them know where we were going. Lee McPhee of Sault Ste. Marie, Ontario, the lodge cook, served us coffee and rice crisp cake. We left word with him that we would stop in again on our way out in a week or ten days. Earlier that morning we had left a cache of extra food on the north shore to retrieve on our return from Hinde.

We soon headed on down the Dubuant River, camping overnight about three miles south of the 61st parallel. The next morning dawned bright and clear. It was an enjoyable ride down those final fourteen miles of rushing water into Hinde Lake. Right after lunch we headed to the west shore where Bob Voss had told us we would find the ruins dug out in the side of an esker. We were soon disappointed to see that the entire west shore of the lake had been burned over in those fires of the previous year. Paddling into the bay where Bob had put an X on our Hinde Lake map, we put ashore. We began to wonder. There was no esker visible from the bay. Only hills of 150 to 200 feet and covered with dead trees and rocks of all sizes. Once more we checked the map. We were definitely in the bay with his X. We began to climb the hill, Darrell going to the right and I to the left searching. Even though the fire would have burned everything, we did expect to find a place in the hillside where a man-made space had been dug out. We agreed to meet back at the canoes ninety minutes later, which we did. But search in vain, high and low, neither of us turned up a clue.

"We must be in the wrong bay," Darrell remarked. I agreed. We paddled north following the shoreline as close as possible. No esker came into view until we came to the one showing on our maps running along the north shore of Hinde Lake. This was encouraging. Disembarking we continued the search. Darrell walking along the esker edge slope near shore and I on top, parallel to each other. We covered nearly two miles along the twenty to thirty foot high ridge. Still we found nothing.

Darrell looks out of an old trapper's cabin: Hinde Lake

Moose stroll near our tent above Hinde Lake.

Paddling to the northeast corner of western Hinde we did find three old log trappers' cabins that most likely had not been used during the last forty or fifty years. Camping overnight behind a sand beach nearby, we discussed the situation and made our plans of procedure for the next day. Darrell checked the GPS. Our coordinates were 61.108 north and 103.419 west. Then it was search and search some more into every little bay and up on every small hill but always finding nothing. What a letdown! Now we asked ourselves, could it be that the place never existed? Or did the fires of '98 burn and cover it with ashes? Was the place a figment of Bob Voss's imagination? Or is Bob Voss an equivocator of the truth? We would likely never know.

Disappointed, we nosed the canoes back into the river and began the long climb upstream. We estimated the time it would require to move up into Wholdaia Lake to be at least five days. It was a pleasant surprise when three days later we had scratched and portaged our way up into Wholdaia. Often the paddles hit rock in mid-stroke as we pushed our way against the speeding Dubuant. Many times the canoes hit bottom to be shoved or pried off the rocks. Paddles were often used as poles while shoving our way along. Many times the only way to proceed was to wade or hop from rock to rock, pulling the loaded canoes along with a rope while trying to keep our balance. Our paddle blades were worn shorter by more than an inch from the beating they had taken from the climb out of Hinde. On two occasions Darrell was able to power paddle his way up along the edge of rapids where my old muscles and waning stamina just couldn't make it. Both times he came back to work my Monarch up, while I walked along on shore.

Wildlife was plentiful below Wholdaia Lake. We often saw eagles, swans, otters and moose. Darrell chased and nearly caught up with one bull moose swimming across the river.

For the sake of brevity, four days later once more we were crossing the long trail between Flett and Selwyn Lakes. All of our equipment, except for the canoes, was moved to a camping area near Selwyn. The tents were set as rain was moving in. An hour later with the showers past, we walked back to Flett for the canoes. Following the usual procedure, Darrell lifted the bow of my canoe as I stepped under and shouldered it. Then he picked up his canoe and led the way along the trail. This time he was going to move on to our campsite and prepare supper. I had moved along the trail for more than a mile. I decided to stop for a brief rest. I needed to find a place where I could set the bow of the canoe on a large rock or tree branch where I could easily get back under after the breather. Moving along above Sacred Lake I saw a big boulder beside the trail. It was seven or eight feet tall with a narrow top. Stepping toward it while looking up as the bow settled on the boulder top, I took the final step, stubbed my toe on a smaller rock I had not seen, and fell crashing into the huge boulder as the canoe went rolling to the ground.

A young bull looks us in the eye

By the time I had picked myself up, Darrell had heard the crash from about a hundred yards ahead and came running back, after putting his canoe down, hollering, "Are you all right Dad?"

"Yup." After explaining what had happened I added, "But I do have a broken rib or two and a banged up knee. I can make it through if you'll help to get it up on my shoulder again."

We were once more underway about five minutes later and eventually made it into camp. While eating supper I recalled the warning given by Chief Leon

Cook the previous year. While speaking of the Great Spirit he had said, "HE gets angry when outsiders walk around up there."

To which Darrell commented, "HE must be angry because we came through here again this year. HE may have decided to punish you so you will stay away in the future. I hope nothing else goes wrong before we can get away from here in the morning."

The next morning with my sore rib and badly swollen knee, we limped and lugged things down the final quarter mile to Selwyn. Paddling was no major problem so we moved on to the south with a strong north wind pushing us along. Two hours later we were approaching the big part of the lake. The seas were rolling too high for us so we cut to the east and into the bay with the abandoned village we had visited two years earlier.

Waiting for an abatement of the powerful wind, we again explored the old settlement. Such a beautiful place even now, with all of the people gone. We walked around with cameras in hand, imagining the activities going on there about a century earlier. Now, many of the old homes have rotted down and some have good-sized trees growing up through where the dirt floors used to be. With no letup in the wind we set up camp and crawled into sleeping bags early.

A strong breeze was blowing from the northwest as we shoved away from shore the next morning at 5:15. An hour later we were bouncing about on the open waters. Hanging in there for another two and a half hours as wind velocity

Camp near south end of Flett to Selwyn trail

grew stronger, we finally sought shelter on the downwind side of an island in mid-lake. The only place to put ashore was on a lengthy pile of all shapes and sizes of rocks. While walking and wobbling my way over the boulder field to a level area near the top, I lost my balance. Reaching out with my right arm I crashed into a large boulder, injuring my shoulder.

Darrell spoke up as he saw it happen. "Oh, no! You've broken your rotator cuff!" He knew the feeling, having had a similar experience as he slipped on a sloping rock in Kabinakagami Lake, Ontario in autumn of 1988.

"Do you think you'll be able to paddle?"

"Don't know how well, but I'll give it a try."

"You sit down there on your cushion while I look over this island to see if I can find a spot to set up the tent. I'm afraid you're not up to paddling." He left, returning fifteen minutes later saying, "It doesn't look good, but there's a spot up on the hill big enough for your tent. Now let's see if you can paddle." With that Darrell helped steady me down over the rocks to the Monarch, holding it as I stepped in and seated myself. He handed me my paddle. Resting the tip of the blade on a rock, I pushed off with my left hand. Then gripping the paddle with both hands, I tried to take a stroke. "Ouch!" Trying again with the blade on the left, I was unable to raise the handle enough to get the blade into the water.

"Don't drift too far away," said Darrell. With my left hand I worked the canoe back to the rock. "Here's what we're going to do," he spoke while helping me out of the Monarch, "I'll put the spray skirt on my canoe and paddle on to the Lodge. If Gordon's there, we'll come back with one of his boats and pick you up. I should make it down there in a couple of hours."

"You'll have to be careful in those big waves."

As he paddled away, he said "I can make it and we'll be back just as soon as possible."

Watching for a few minutes, I didn't like what I was seeing as he moved away from the island into those heavy seas. He bounced along over each swell and soon completely disappeared from view.

Now I had time to do some serious thinking. Why, I wondered, did we have to go to Hinde Lake? And why did Leon Cook caution me about the fact that the Great Spirit of the Chipewyan's does not like outsiders messing around Sacred Lake? We may have made their Great Spirit angry! First my broken rib and now, a broken shoulder! Finally I was getting the message! Certainly, I vowed, if we can get away from here this time, I will certainly never return!

Five hours later a motor boat was heading my way. Gordon Wallace was at the controls. Thank God! Darrell had made it and I was being rescued. They soon had me seated in the boat; everything, including my canoe, was loaded and we were underway.

An hour later we were on the dock in front of the Lodge. While walking up the trail to the Lodge, I saw an old man with a cane limping down to meet me. Soon I recognized the old fellow. It was none other than Bob Voss. Apparently he had heard we were returning from Hinde Lake. We greeted each other and he asked only one question. "I've been wondering if you found that old cabin I told you about?"

"Yes," I replied "It's still there." I stood there expecting him to ask if we had found the Japanese communications setup he had previously talked so much about, but he turned and walked away. In disbelief I walked into the Lodge. Mary Wallace, extended her usual, friendly greeting and asked if I would like an ice pack for my injured shoulder. Being very chilly, I declined. Gordon contacted Points North after assigning us a nice room. The hot shower warmed me as I cleaned up a little but could use only my left hand. Lots of good food, friendship and hospitality continued until we flew away the next morning.

Mr. Voss managed to keep out of our sight during the remaining hours of our visit. Certainly Darrell and I have been the cause of many, many hearty laughs during and since our journey down north to Hinde Lake. Certainly both of us have finally learned a valuable lesson. Namely—Don't always believe everything you hear! The two of us are now likely known all across central Canada and the Territories as "that gullible pair of paddlers from Michigan."

To be fair to Mr. Voss in retrospect, we must say he is a very likable gentleman. He is a wonderful storyteller and a spinner of some whopping yarns. We really liked him and still think many good thoughts about him. In fact, had it not been for Bob Voss, Darrell and I would have completely missed out on those wonderful canoe excursions we enjoyed in 1998 and 1999. "Thank you, Bob!"

18

A Lake Can Be A River

The millennium year of 2000 rolled in. The planning for this book was underway. It still had no title but certainly it was going to contain the Selwyn Lake saga as well as more on the life of wilderness master, Ragnar Jonsson. Needing more information on Mr. Jonsson plus photos of his Nueltin Lake environs inspired us to go back to Nueltin and check it out.

La Ronge Air, out of Lynn Lake, dropped us off on the shore of Shannon Lake, some thirty miles south of Nueltin on June 30. We would be moving through part of an area familiar to Mr. Jonsson during his forty-three years around Nueltin.

On the second day of paddling we entered Shannon's outlet, the Seaman River. We soon learned to proceed with caution after taking a lapfull of water over the bow while descending one of the river's many rapids. Along the way the dorsal fins of arctic grayling frequently broke the surface. Had we been fishing, we could have killed some time there. We did portage two of the major drops, one of these is known as Hleethelteedayeezhi Rapids. By evening we had arrived and were looking out across the tip of Nueltin's southeastern arm. We were still in Manitoba and planned to paddle to the northwest corner of the 120-

mile long Nueltin Lake in search of Windy River Post, once operated by the Hudson's Bay Company and later by the Fred Schweder family.

On July 4, a perfectly gorgeous summer day, we pushed along to the northwest for twenty-eight miles crossing the 60th parallel. For the first time, we set foot in the recently created Territory of Nunavut. Climbing the esker behind our camp during the evening, to the north we could see solid pack ice extending all across the lake. However, the next morning we were pleasantly surprised to be able to squeeze through an opening in the ice near the island along the eastern shore.

Then moving along north and west through the lake's narrows, we stopped at Nueltin Fly-in Lodge Narrows camp. Invited in by manager Bob Schultz, we were treated to coffee and muffins by his wife Barb. Discussing the situation, Bob told us, "There's still a lot of ice up that way so you're not going to go much farther."

Moving north again with an east wind blowing, we kept near the eastern shore. Ravines still had huge piles of the previous winter's snow along their southern slopes. Soon ice appeared ahead. Our chances of reaching Windy River Post began to dim. We had proceeded only another eight miles when we arrived at the edge of the ice. Finding a place to go ashore and walking to a nearby hilltop we were dismayed at the view. With clear skies and good visibility, look-

Ragnar's initials on the slope of Monument Point

Ragnar's gravesite on Jonsson Island

ing north to the horizon toward Smith Bay, it was solid ice. Looking east into Hearne Bay—solid ice. Looking to the northwestern shore across the bay we had just moved out of—solid ice from shore to shore!

Discussing the situation and recalling our long wait for the ice to melt in Yathkyed Lake as we descended the Kazan River many years before, our decision was almost immediate and unanimous. We could not wait for the meltdown. We would turn back.

On the following day, after another brief stop at Narrows' Lodge, we moved into the narrowest part of Nueltin Lake. An island is located in the center with fast moving water flowing down along both sides. Paddling along close to the right shore, we turned on the power as we entered the down speeding water. Soon Darrell was moving forward a foot or so with each stroke of his paddle while my speed steadily decreased. Now I was gaining only an inch or two per stroke. This is where I learned that a lake can also be a river. Who would have expected this? In the middle of Nueltin Lake, to find several inches of a drop—nearly a foot!

Running low on energy, I soon gave it up, floating back down with the rushing water. Darrell continued to dig, still gaining a little with each powerful stroke and had soon disappeared into a little bay above. I tried to work my way up along the other side of the island. The result was the same. Now I had only one choice. I would portage everything over the island if I could only find a place to put ashore. While searching for the best spot, I heard a call. It was my partner, who had put ashore in the little bay and walked back to ask if he could paddle my Monarch up for me. Certainly he could. Then I walked across the brushy tundra and was soon back in my canoe, thankful indeed to have Darrell nearby to help.

Two days later we paddled in to a beach on the east side of Jonsson Island. We soon located Ragnar Jonnson's gravesite with its plaque near the tip of the nearby peninsula. We also found his old teepee still standing in a clump of spruce and tamarack trees, with open door, plus a pile of fishnets, empty bottles and a few cans. Jonnson Island has an esker running its entire length, mainly covered with caribou moss, bear berries, and some widely spaced trees around its seven small lakes with flowers everywhere. We camped overnight enjoying the great scenery. Our only problem—black flies by the thousands!

Helped along by the north wind the next day, we made a stop to see the remains of another of Ragnar's old teepees. This one was on the island where Debbie and I had spent a day with him in 1983. The teepee had collapsed into a pile. Now no whiskey jacks chattered in the nearby trees.

Later in the afternoon we arrived at the former Tree Line Lodge. We contacted La Ronge Air and they would pick us up the following day. Camping over on Big Sand Beach we had a pleasant surprise at six o'clock the next morning. A Chipewyan guide from the lodge motored to an island off the beach to feed his dogs. Seeing us on the beach he stopped in for a brief visit. He was Ovide Denecheze, who has lived near Nueltin all of his life. This fifty-nine-year-old guide told us he had indeed paddled with Ragnar to Brochet the summer he was sixteen. Ovide said he never attended school a day in his life; the year he was to be flown out to The Pas, the school burned down. He has taught himself to speak English, to read and to write. He and his wife have raised eight children in a cabin only a few miles north of Big Sand Beach.

While waiting for our aircraft at the new Nueltin Fly-in Lodge, the former Tree Line Lodge, we visited with owners Shawn Gurke and his mom, Lois. We also enjoyed a chat with the Lodge's pilot, Myron Ridley. He told us about Ilse Schweder, the girl Ragnar had rescued after she had been lost on Nueltin Lake ice for nine days, many winters before. Mr. Ridley also spoke of other early history of the area, giving us much to ponder as we headed for home, where we surprised everyone by our brief absence.

19

Bushed In the Bush

Disappointed about our failing to reach Windy River Post, Darrell and I would make one more attempt in July of 2001. This time we laid out a different route, a route where ice should be no problem. Aware of the old cliché "Beaten Paths are For Beaten Men," we chose a route that would definitely get us off the "Beaten Path." Little did we know just how beaten we were to become. This time we would paddle from Fort Hall Lake down the Thlewiaza River to a place where we could portage over into the Putahow River. We would follow it down across Putahow Lake, to portage into Charlie Lake. Then north through a chain of ten small tundra lakes into the Poor Fish River and follow it down to Windy Lake and River to the old Windy River Post. From there it would be south to Nueltin Fly-in Lodge.

From Points North we were flown on July 4 to a beach in southeastern Fort Hall Lake and paddled the five miles to set up camp at the narrows. This was the place where the four of us had camped in 1968 as written in ***Cold Summer Wind*** and also the spot where Debbie and I had set our tent in 1982. Before calling it a day we walked along the edge of the esker to once more visit Chief Kasmere's grave. There had been many changes since our earlier visits as the whole area all the way to Kasmere Lake was burned over by the fire of 1991. Now only two separate carved little boards lying flat on the ground remain to mark the Chief's gravesite.

By noon of the second day we arrived at the north end of Thanout Lake and were searching for the Old North Trail passing Kasmere Falls. Fifteen minutes earlier we had been looking for any remains of the old Fort Hall Post but had found nothing, as the old Post had been completely consumed by the same fire. The trail we were seeking begins out of the little lake west of the falls. Rain overtook us before completing the carry. Our tents went up near trail's end in a downpour. Rain continued overnight and supper consisted of a box of Cracker Jack each.

Then it was on down the Thlewiaza and across Kasmere Lake. Below the lake, as the river turns south into Graves Lake, we continued north and east under sunny skies to make three portages into Gillander Lake and the Putahow River system. Then it was down river through Thuytowayazi Lake and on to Husky Portage. There we had difficulties in finding the trail, which we finally discovered follows the left riverbank for the first half mile, then crosses over the hills north to a bay in southwestern Putahow Lake. Once we located the trail, we moved across in four hours and encamped near the trailhead. A bald eagle flew from a treetop as we arrived with the final carry.

Once settled in above the sand beach, we paddled across the narrow bay to have a look over the esker paralleling the shore. We hoped to find the remains of the home of legendary Eskimo Charlie, the man Ragnar told us about in 1983. Darrell and I had also both read the article by R. H. Cockburn in the Spring 1983 issue of *The Beaver*. There he writes about his findings in the journal of explorer Prentice G. Downes. In 1940 Downes canoed with trapper and trader Alfred Peterson from Brochet to Putahow Lake where they met Eskimo Charlie. Here are a few quotes from *The Beaver:*

> 1 (Eskimo Charlie) came into the North many years ago—about 1907. Among other things, he is known as the greatest [hot air merchant] in the country. He is now over 60.
>
> 2 He has always been known for his fine gardens. B-s'er or not, the fact remains he is an extraordinarily ingenious and clever man, with a good mind and is the dirtiest looking human, sartorially and otherwise I have ever seen. The Chipewyans hate him as much as he hates them, which is very considerable.
>
> 3 I was amazed to see what he had done at his place, which was located some distance back from the shore on the other side of the esker.

With this information we knew approximately where to look for anything remaining.

Ashore on the northwest side of the bay, we walked the esker top. Finding no clue we spread out on the return searching the level caribou moss covered plateau. I soon began finding old tree stumps chopped with an axe. Then came a larger stump cut off by a saw. Darrell soon joined me and together we came upon the place where Charlie's buildings and garden once stood. We found his old cook stove, teapot, granite dish, pail and the sole of a rubber boot. His garden area with an irrigation ditch through the center is now growing healthy looking grass—a grass we found only in his garden, which judging from its luxuriant growth, must have been well fertilized until his death in 1944.

A perfect morning followed a good night's sleep inside the tents and away from the hungry hoard of insects. Fog was lifting into clear blue sky as we paddled out of the bay just before sunrise to cross Putahow Lake. Our route took us mainly to the north, northeast passing many islands and into the northernmost bay of the lake. By midday we were making the three portages following the ancient trails over into Charlie Lake. An hour later, crossing the 60th parallel, we entered Nunavut Territory pushing along to the extreme northwest corner of Charlie. There we called it a day knowing from our maps there would be two lengthy portages to negotiate on the morrow.

The next morning, unable to find any sort of trail, we headed to the north carrying our backpacks plus smaller packs in each hand. It was a full mile to the next lake. The entire area had burned over about fifteen years before, leaving dead trees now mostly toppled every which way. Picking our way over and around the deadfalls, rocks and bushes, across hills and hollows was a rough go. The black flies were everywhere—the most we had ever seen. At one time I was unable to see anything with my left eye so I asked my partner to look and see what was wrong. He looked saying, "Your eye is full of blood!" Wiping it with my glove, blood did cover the tip of my finger. A black fly had bitten after crawling into the corner of my eye. Those black little devils were continually getting under my glasses, in my mouth, ears and nose by the dozens, even with my headnet on.

It was a tough go to the next lake. I fell four times with my backpack on but was uninjured. Darrell fell only once, ripping his trousers and tearing his skin on the sharp stub of a broken deadfall. By the time we had dragged the canoes across and made the third trip with the food and other packs, the day was nearly gone. Paddling a half-mile to the west shore of the little lake we set up camp. We were both really bushed. In fact, double bushed, as we were bushed in the bush.

There were nine more of these small lakes to negotiate before arriving at an expansion of the Poor Fish River. In reading Sidney A. Keighley's book ***Trader,***

Tripper, Trapper we had previously learned we would be on the route to Hudson's Bay Company's old Poor Fish Lake Post. Mr. Keighley had been in charge of the Post there in 1928 and '29. He had written, "There were thirty portages in the thirty-five miles between Putahow and Poor Fish Lakes." The Poor Fish Lake Post was closed in 1932. This is the reason we were finding no trails. There are none, as no one had needed to use those trails in nearly seventy years. So—here we were, right where we had thought we wanted to be, well off the beaten path!

Then came five days of struggling, suffering and sweating with daytime temperatures up to 88° F as we moved through those little lakes, with trailless carries between. Our route was continuously choked with gnarled willows, tamarack and decaying birch as we moved around the rocks and over the hills. We found black flies by the millions all along the way with plenty of mosquitoes, deer flies and bulldogs, too. On one of the portages, feeling something in my right ear, automatically I stuck my finger up to the ear to brush away whatever it was. As my finger touched my ear, I heard a 'pop' sound, like the sound of a breaking balloon inside the ear. Glancing at my finger, it was covered with blood. The blood spattered on the brim of my hat and down the side of my face. I picked out the remains of a deer fly and continued on toward the next lake. We were indeed double bushed on those evenings.

At each of those lakes as the canoes were loaded, I would quickly paddle out from shore into any breeze available, swing my hat to slap at the black fly throng, lay the paddle across the gunwales, then jerk off my headnet with one hand while still swinging my hat with the other. On one occasion, as I jerked the headnet, my prescription glasses caught on the net, falling into the lake. Fortunately, I did have an old set of spectacles in my pack.

Solitary sandpipers were plentiful along the shores of each of these lakes. A solitary bird was certain to fly out to meet us whenever we neared the shore of each lake. The bird would continue its shrill, noisy and unending *weet-weet-weet-weet* until we had passed their nesting area.

On July 15, following a mile long difficult carry, we arrived in a larger lake. Now we were in an expansion of the Poor Fish River system. Then came an exciting ride down rapids after rapids. Darrell visually checked out each of these before I followed him through. In all, there were at least fifteen drops in the river. No major mishaps occurred, however, on two occasions small amounts of water splashed over the bow into our laps. Great sport, but I was too tired and low on energy to really enjoy as we made two more rough portages.

Two days of down river and we arrived at the final rapids where the Poor Fish plunges into southwestern Windy Lake. "It looks like we can make it," my partner called. Following him about three canoe lengths behind, suddenly his canoe swung broadside as he hung on a rock. Rather than plowing into him with the bow of my craft, I swung to the left but too late to miss him. We broadsided, still in an upright position, hanging there with those tons of water pouring under us. Darrell was soon able to break loose leaving me still hanging. At that instant we discovered another major problem. Now the rudders of the two canoes were locked together. What to do? We were in mid-river. Nearly a quarter mile of this set of rapids still rolled ahead of us. Looking at the problem, Darrell asked me to try to move a foot or two forward as he pushed his craft back against the current. Then wiggling the controls, he eventually broke free heading on down. Still hanging there, after a few minutes of maneuvering, fortunately, I floated free and headed on down to Windy Lake where, with camera in hand, my partner sat waiting for me.

Moving across Windy Lake next day we made a stop to inspect the remains of the old Revillon Frères Post along the western shore. This post opened in the mid 1920's to serve the Inuit from Ennadai Lake and the Kazan as well as the Chipewyans. At that time this was right in the heart of the area containing countless valuable fur-bearing animals. Some artifacts of the old post's equipment still lay scattered about, including a set of platform scales and a pair of Lapp skis. We wondered if they once belonged to Ragnar.

Back in the '20s competition arrived in full force in Windy country. The HBC (Hudson's Bay Company) went into business near the junction of the Red and Windy Rivers. Several white traders and trappers opened posts. Some of those were Cecil "Husky" Harris, Del Simons and I. H.'Windy' Smith. Then over at Poor Fish Lake the HBC opened the post operated by Sidney Keighley.

Remains of Del Simon's or Simons, Ltd. Post in 2001

The remains of Windy River Post in 2001

This was done to intercept the Inuit on their way to the more distant places to trade. Competition in the area was indeed a competitive venture. By the early '30s and during the Great Depression those vast numbers of fur-bearing animals steadily declined. All but the HBC and Revillon Frères posts were closed. In 1936 the HBC bought out Revillon leaving only one—the Nueltin Lake Post—and that survived until 1941. Fred Schweder then built the Windy River Post.

Upon entering Windy River with a thunderstorm moving in, we cut short our search for the old Nueltin Lake Post near the junction of the Red River. Then looking to the right as we entered Simons Lake, an old building came into view. We had found the remains of the Del Simons or Simons Ltd. Post. Only one log structure still stands; the roof caved in but the walls are completely upright.

Around the bend at the lower end of Simons Lake the river once more pinched in between the hills. We could hear the throaty rumble ahead, so once more I pulled in behind to follow my guide down those rapids. This time I maintained an extra canoe length behind. We did not need another canoe crash. The next one could end in disaster.

Camping over on a barren rocky hillside, the next morning we continued on down the river. An east wind picked up shortly after sunrise. Now it was rapids after rapids around each bend. On two occasions we chose to portage our way through the small trees and bushes, around rocks, over the hills and across the rough tundra. On one occasion, as we returned for the canoes, a cow moose stood directly across the river watching our every move.

By noon we arrived at Windy River Post, took photos of the remains and imagined how the place must have looked back in the 1940s when it also served as the home of the Fred Schweder family. We had a quick lunch and paddled out across Windy Bay to the outpost of Nueltin Lake Fly-in Lodge. Welcomed ashore by hosts Jerry and Michelle, we enjoyed ice-cold pop as we chatted and the east wind howled on. These were the first people we had seen in the two weeks since leaving Kasmere Lake. Then paddling east into the wind, we struggled along near the foot of Josie's Hill looking for a place to camp. The seas were much too high for us out on Smith Bay. After more than two hours of pushing into the near gale, we found a barren hilltop near the east end of the long island in Windy Bay. Once the tents were set we began to relax. There were few insects. The wind was holding them at bay. With clear skies we anticipated a drop in the wind before morning. Little did we know, we were about to be windbound in Windy Bay. The gale from the east continued and early the next morning came a downpour of cold rain. With the temperature at 42° F and the blasts of wind coming directly across the barrens and off the ice of northern Hudson Bay, we were forced to remain inside our sleeping bags for any comfort. The tents did shake and rattle with each succeeding blast—but fortunately they did not roll. It's amazing just how much punishment a good Eureka tent can withstand. The blowing rain continued without letup for the next two days. On the second day, my journal reads, "More of the same—only worse! The 'Cold Summer Wind' blows on! Powerful gusts with a steady downpour of rain until late afternoon. Darrell fixed us a quick supper. Then back into the tents to keep warm." This storm served as a reminder about our 'Pledge to the North,' signed in July of 1978 as recorded in the book ***Cold Summer Wind*** and also inside a rock cairn along the lower Back River.

Early on the third morning the wind eased off as it swung to the northwest and Old Sol decided to send down some of its glory. We broke camp in haste, eager to move south on Nueltin. Three days later we once more visited Jonsson Island. We wanted to find Ragnar's old log cabin, the only one he ever built. We found no trace of it. His teepee, however, was still intact. Late in the afternoon Darrell made a phone call from his canoe seat to Points North to let them know we expected to arrive at the former Tree Line Lodge the following afternoon. The call was made using the Globestar Satellite phone. That's progress!

We slid the canoes onto the beach at Nueltin Fly-in Lodge just before noon on July 25. Darrell again called Points North while standing there on the beach to report our arrival. He learned they would be able to pick us up the next day. I was eager to again talk with Ovide Denecheze, to inquire more about his acquaintance with Ragnar. Talking with Gary Gurke at the lodge, I learned that

Ovide was guiding for the day at Seal Hole Lake but would return in the evening. We pitched our tents near the beach, waiting and relaxing. We dined with the staff and the food and fellowship were excellent.

When Ovide and his group of fishermen returned from Seal Hole, he agreed to meet us for breakfast in the Lodge at five the next morning. We walked in at 5:05 and Ovide was waiting. A lady sitting next to him was introduced as his wife, Mary. We soon learned Mrs. Denecheze works at the Lodge and speaks very little English. Ovide graciously answered all of my questions. The big surprise came when I told him about my reading of the book ***Sleeping Island*** by Prentiss G. Downes. When Mr. Downes canoed to Nueltin Lake in 1939 he had found a man to guide him to the HBC Post at the confluence of the Red and Windy Rivers. "Is there any chance," I asked, "that when you were a young lad, did you know a fellow who lived around here by the name of Zebedeeze?" The whole room lighted up. Huge smiles instantly appeared on both Ovide's and Mary's faces.

"Yes!" said Ovide as he grinned at Mary. "Zebedeeze was Mary's father!"

In the afternoon we were picked up by Points North and headed for home.

Ovide Denecheze

20

The Rescue

During our visit to Nueltin Fly-In Lodge in 2000 we heard talk of the young girl from Windy River Post whose life was saved by Ragnar Jonsson many years before. The story was that he had found a daughter of Fred Schweder lying out on the ice of Nueltin Lake in mid-winter. From a distance he thought he was looking at a dead caribou or possibly a bear. He went out to investigate and found the girl nearly frozen to death. He carried her to his teepee and warmed her up, giving her some food and tea. Knowing who she was, a few days later he returned her to Windy River Post.

We thought this strange, wondering why Ragnar had not mentioned this to us during those days we spent with him in 1983. Apparently he was just too unboastful and modest to talk about one of the most important things accomplished during his entire lifetime.

Intrigued by the rescue, I wanted to secure the details and include the correct facts. Myron Ridley, a pilot at Nueltin Lodge, told me the Schweder girl's name was Elsie and he believed she lived in Thompson, Manitoba. In September, I checked with the telephone system for the number of any Schweder living in Thompson. There were none listed. Realizing Elsie Schweder was likely now married and going by her husband's family name, I wondered how to find her. I checked at Churchill for a Charles or Fred Schweder. Again, no success.

In late April of 2001 I received a note from Ronald L. Craven of Pine River,

Minnesota, who had recently read ***Cold Summer Wind***. He had enjoyed the book and especially the part about Ragnar Jonsson. He later told me he had visited Nueltin Lake and the old Windy River Post. Mr. Craven was also an acquaintance of the former Ilse (not Elsie) Schweder, the girl rescued by Ragnar in 1946. He put me in touch and I soon began corresponding with Ilse and her husband, Bryan Clements.

Mrs. Clements supplied me with an article from the *Winnipeg Free Press* written by Bob Lowery. She also sent an article written by R. Stephen Irwin, M.D., about the times he had met with Ragnar while sport fishing at Nueltin Lake in the 1970s.

Here is what actually occurred: Charles Schweder, the eldest son of Fred Schweder of Windy River Post, was going to his trap line in the Kazan River-Ennadai Lake Area. It was early in March of 1946. Fred, Jr., Ilse and the two younger brothers, Mike and Norman decided to accompany Charles on the trip. This made three sleds: Charles and his team, Fred with his team and fourteen-year-old Ilse with her toboggan and team of pups. There were two cabins between the Post at Windy River and Charles' trap line. These were simple, overnight shelters, log-frame with canvas roofs and a stove. The distance to Charles' cabin on Kazan River from Windy River Post was about eighty miles.

They overnighted in Charles' cabin. The next day they had a lovely day near Ennadai Lake and Ilse remembers the kids chasing ground squirrels on the esker. The next morning the weather started to change and Charles said they should get going so they would make it to the first cabin before the impending storm hit. Charles was staying behind to check his traps.

Arriving at the first cabin, the weather was still good so they decided to carry on to the next cabin. When they were about halfway there the weather struck and they were immediately in a whiteout. They were soon separated, but Fred turned back and found Ilse. At this point they decided to put the two young boys on Fred's sled and they tied Ilse's team to Fred's sled with the check line.

They set off again and were going along nicely until Fred made a sharp turn and the check line broke. Ilse was now on her own in a whiteout with no control over her dogs. She could not even see her lead dog for the blowing snow. She only had the inexperienced young dogs. A good experienced team would have found their way to the cabin.

Ilse had no idea which way to go, and immediately was lost. The dogs kept going, mainly heading away from the strong blasts of the north wind. At one point the toboggan turned over and her bedroll went bouncing away, over the hard packed snow. She had nothing to survive with. In talking about it later, Ilse said, "All I had was my gray blanket and a little teakettle. And worst of all, I had no matches, no food, no gun and no knife."

Ilse Schweder Clements was fourteen years old in 1946

Her dogs kept going and soon became hungry. They went out of control and would chase after any ptarmigan or caribou. According to her brothers who searched for her later, Ilse passed within yards of the old Hudson's Bay Post near Windy Lake. They were able to follow her crooked trail for a ways after the storm subsided late the next day. She crossed the Red River, falling through the ice, but made it to the other side. With frozen feet she carried on but the dogs were totally out of control. She suffered on for four days but when the dogs got themselves stuck in the trees in a ravine she abandoned them.

The next morning, not knowing where she was, Ilse set out on frozen feet. The caribou had been moving north. With their trails to follow she decided to follow them south, hoping to meet up with some of the Dene people. She needed food. The only thing she found to eat were cranberries, which protruded from the snow in the wooded gullies. These she gathered and carried along in the teakettle. She would soon have to find some more substantial food. She recalls that every day she became more and more tired and had an ever-increasing longing for both food and sleep. "Every time I went to sleep, I wondered whether I'd ever wake up again."

Eventually she came out on Nueltin Lake. Going along one day in the distance she saw the big rock that she realized was the huge rock on Ragnar Jonsson's Island. Now she knew where she was. Walking across to the island, she lay down to rest.

It had been nine days since the blizzard and she had walked about ninety miles over rough terrain with frozen feet. Hungry and exhausted, she had kept going eating only cranberries and snow. A rifle shot woke her up and she could see someone out on the lake that had just shot a caribou. As luck would have it, the hunter was Ragnar. He was coming back to his cabin, and he would pass right by her. Soon his pups, which ran loose, found her. He drew his rifle thinking she was a bear, so she stood. When he got to her he could see she was in bad shape. Her fingers and hands were badly cut from falling on ice and rocks. She was so very thin, just skin and bones.

Ragnar built a fire right there and made tea, which Ilse sipped. He gave her a sleeping robe to wrap around her, while he boiled the fresh caribou tongue. He offered it to her but she didn't want to eat it. He pitched his tent close by, and she went in and went to sleep. The next morning, Ragnar broke camp, and they started back to the Schweders' house at the mouth of Windy River. They traveled all that day and night. Then late the following morning they arrived home, however, no one was there. A note with some fresh baked bread said, "We're all out looking for Ilse!"

Mrs. Clements now says, "Mr. Jonsson was so worried about my feet, which were frozen black. It took six months for my feet to heal. I'm so grateful that he saved my life!"

The Schweder family, except for Charles and Fred, Jr., left Windy River for good that spring because of Ilse's frozen feet. Heading for the south, they hauled their freighter canoe on a dogsled over the ice until finding open water on Nueltin Lake.

Ilse Schweder and Ragnar became long-time friends even though seldom seeing each other. They did meet once when he paddled across northern Manitoba to Churchill. She was with him again at his funeral in The Pas on July 1, 1988 when his friends decided to take his ashes to Jonsson Island. They brought along a wheelbarrow, cement and construction tools to build a cairn of boulders on the crest of a prominent point overlooking the beach not far from his teepee.

21

Windy River Post

While corresponding with Bryan and Ilse Clements in autumn 2001, they asked if I had read the book ***When the Foxes Ran*** by Gerry Dunning. Earlier the reading of this book had been suggested to me by Ron Craven, Bill Layman and Lynda Holland. Being unable to find a copy on the Internet, I called one of my old friends, Lorraine Brandson, Editor of *Eskimo Magazine* and curator of the Eskimo Museum in Churchill, Manitoba. Polar bears were moving through the settlement at the time and she was busy with tourists in town. However, she had the book in stock and took the time to send me a copy.

It is a wonderful read for anyone interested in the rich history of the area along the western side of Hudson Bay during the fur trading years. Gerry Dunning interviewed six of the old time trappers and trappers' wives who were living in Churchill in the early 1980s. He writes the stories of each, as told to him. One real surprise to me is the story told by Francis Voisey who is the daughter of Cecil "Husky" Harris. Gerry Dunning is a nephew of Mrs. Voisey. "Husky" Harris was one of the earlier white trappers and traders of the area.

Charles Schweder, older brother of Ilse Schweder, is another of the people written up in ***When the Foxes Ran.*** With the author's permission, here is a somewhat condensed version from this book in the words recorded by Mr. Schweder about his life around Windy River Post.

I was born at Reindeer Lake near Rapid River in 1925. Reindeer, where we lived, was a trading centre and a storage place for freight. The freight came in by horses during the winter months from Prince Albert, Saskatchewan, to be stored in a warehouse. It was my father's job (Fred Schweder) to deliver it when the lake opened up. The Trading Post, owned by the Hudson's Bay Company, consisted of our family. A trapper and few other people lived across the river. We had five boys and four girls in our family. I was the oldest and our daily life was pretty much an outdoor life.

We never really traveled anywhere, just stayed at the Post. If we went somewhere in the winter it was by dog team and summertime travel was by canoe.

I didn't start school until we moved to The Pas, Manitoba, where I attended Public School. I guess my father moved to The Pas to have a change in life and to give the kids some sort of schooling. I also picked up some schooling at Birch Hills.

In 1939 our family left The Pas to go back north. The Depression forced us north. Bread might have been only five cents a loaf and rent $12.00 per month but our family couldn't make ends meet in town. As well, a mink was worth $8.00, and for $8.00 at The Pas, you could buy one heck of a lot of groceries.

We went back to Reindeer Lake, then headed north to Ennadai Lake. Dad was trading for Revillon Frères then. Our whole family went north—Mom, Dad,

Remains of Windy River Post from ridge behind in 2001

myself, Anne, Fred, Mary, Ilse, Norman, Theresa, Mike and Robert. We went north with two twenty-foot canoes. The trip took around three weeks as we camped every night, setting up a tent. We arrived at the Post and imagine this— "We got out of one of the canoes, and the fellow my father's relief jumps in and heads south." He didn't even spend the night with us. So we took over the Post and his dog team. I remember his dogs took quite a while to get used to. When we went north, my father planned to stay three years but we ended up staying eleven.

Our family adjusted quite easily to the Post. My father was a man who liked to rise early and was like that until the day he died. Six A.M. was his rising time and he'd always give us a yell to get up. You have to remember that we were all just kids in those days so I was a lazy bugger, too. I'll always remember Pop in the mornings. He'd yell, "Hey, it's seven o'clock! Isn't anyone getting up around here?" Now when it's seven o'clock, I'm yelling at my own kids.

People might wonder what we did to keep busy, but there was never really a slack hour. We'd always check our nets in the morning then bring the fish in. We never fed the dogs until around noon hour. Afternoons you'd chop wood, haul water, and work around the post. My father did all the cooking and once a month we'd have a large bake up—bread, pies and buns. Gosh, he made good pies.

For entertainment we listened to the radio that was powered by our windmill. My favorite programs were ***Amos and Andy*** and ***Woodhouse and Hawkins.*** CKY in Winnipeg was my favorite station. Our radio sometimes pulled in Finland or Tokyo, however, the northern lights affected the reception at times.

My mother was a Cree Indian and very Catholic. My father was German and Protestant, yet when they were married all the kids were raised Catholic. My father never changed over and died a Protestant. At Reindeer Lake, there was a presence of the R.C. Church but after we moved north, the Church held little importance. A few priests came into our area but they really made little headway.

At home our family only spoke English, even though my mother spoke Cree and my father German. It's too bad we were never taught their languages. We had to learn some Inuit over the next few years as well.

My mother died when Robert was still in diapers. The second year we went north, all the girls were left behind, so only Fredie, Norman, Mike and myself went back north with Dad. The girls were raised by the nuns at Sifton, Manitoba and Norman was later sent to school. Dad paid for them to stay and have their schooling and you could say he probably had some problems trying to keep things going. My sisters hated the convent life as the nuns put them to work and never paid them for anything, even during the summers. We had some hard times like anyone else but, somehow, we got by the best we could.

As far as trading up north went, Dad worked for Revillon Frères, then when the Hudson's Bay bought Revillon Frères out, he worked for the Bay at their Nueltin Lake Post until he finally went independent. Trading provided a living and that's all. No one ever got rich up north but we ate good and had few worries. No one starved! Maybe some years we made good money but other years we'd have to scrape.

Our trade was mainly directly with the inland Eskimos. The Kazan Eskimos were our nearest neighbors—some only sixteen miles away. The first years we picked up a little Inuit but not that much. We never had a language problem though due to the friendliness of these people. The Eskimos came around only long enough to do their trading, have a cup of tea, then they'd be off. We never saw them that much during the first years.

When the Eskimos came in they were paid $8.00 for each white fox. This was the price given to my father by the Hudson's Bay. So Dad would give the Eskimos eight sticks side by side, each representing $1.00. The Eskimo would then buy whatever he wanted. Up north a pound of tea cost $3.00 in those days —imagine that—you could buy it in The Pas for $.50 a pound. Flour went for around $1.00 a pound but what the Eskimos really wanted was ammunition and tea. Tea to them was like beer is to us today. The Eskimos seldom bought sugar, as it was more a luxury item to them. Ammunition, that is lead, powder, and caps was their main purchase because they did their own reloading. We could have long underwear and shirts hanging in the front in the Post, yet they never exchanged for them because they always made their own clothing. Traps were bought from us and they were a costly item at $.50 each. In The Pas traps were a heck of a lot cheaper. It was hard times that probably forced the Eskimos to trap.

All the people up north seemed like good people to me—in a way, quiet people. We learned pretty quickly where each bunch was from, whether they were Cree, Chipewyan, or Inuit. They all had their own peculiar way and their dress would be a little different from one another.

I don't know if the Inuit held any prejudice towards us, maybe a little, however, we always had a good supply of ammunition, tea, matches, and tobacco on hand to trade with them. Later the Eskimos mainly used the 30-30 and 44-40 rifles.

We boys spent almost every summer in Flin Flon while Dad went to Winnipeg with the fur, then he'd visit the girls at Sifton. In the fall we'd head back north with the supplies. Generally we left the Post in April while there was still ice and snow. We'd go by dog team to the south end of Nueltin Lake and leave the dogs there with a Chipewyan Camp. Then we'd canoe down to Flin Flon. The last few years we were up north, we started canoeing through to Churchill, as it was shorter. Eventually we started using planes to Churchill as it was faster than dogs or canoes.

In the summers we seldom traveled anywhere due to the mosquito season. The trips we canoed weren't expensive in or out as gasoline was $.40 a gallon and I had an old 8 horsepower motor that gave us three hundred miles to ten gallons of gas. If we stayed up north for a summer I could travel for months on ten gallons of gas.

My father worked for the Hudson's Bay Company until 1939, then he went on his own. As long as you were with a company, they provided a house. Up north you don't rent anything, you just take an axe, sharpen it, and build. We built our own Post (Windy River Post), hauled in our own supplies and tried to make a go of it as there weren't many traders up there at the time.

We were always busy. We had nets to check, wood to haul, dog harnesses to repair and new sleighs to build. After a few years, Dad quit the trading when everything petered out as the natives down around Brochet died off. Whooping cough and measles came through and didn't they die—"whole camps." When Dad left we brothers, Fredie and I, stayed to trap. The following year, measles hit the Eskimos. My gosh, they died like flies. Their dying put everything down up north for the traders. When people are dying, it's not the trader that's important, it's the people! Why wasn't there help? Oh, the doctors came in one time. Once! Then some sort of laboratory came in. I really don't think they accomplished much. The different diseases killed over one half the people. Those were very sad days for the north.

Imagine this, if you will. A lot of Chipewyan Camps existed between our Post and Brochet. When the sickness came the people would leave one camp for another only to find more sickness. Imagine native people coming to a camp. The tents were there and there would be nobody living. Now that is a sin! No, not a sin, a Crime! A Crime by one civilization against another. Gee Whiz, in one year the Chipewyan tribe was cut in half before Christmas time…! The same thing happened to the Eskimo people. When my father first took us into that country, they were a strong, healthy people, yet disease took them, too.

Our family eventually raised our own dogs. You know, when you raise your own dogs, they won't move for anyone else. My team of six dogs was like that and so was my brother Fredie's. We fed them mainly fish and sometimes caribou.

I started trapping when I was thirteen. At fourteen I was on my own. The first year I trapped close to the Post. One time I brought in four fox skins and got a 44-40 from Dad. Sometimes I'd get eight foxes a day but I gave all my fur to my father. I really had no use for the money but he did. The next year when Fredie and I really got going on our own, things changed. The north taught us to be men at an early age. One time, for example, I was coming from Ennadai Lake when Fredie and I met up. "I got twenty-eight," I told him. "How many did you get?" He said, "About sixty!"

You didn't need to have a registered trapline in those years. For $5.00 a year you could trap anywhere in the territories. I used to trap between Ennadai Lake and Nueltin Lake, an area of about sixty miles in length. Fredie and I built shelters every 10 miles, usually in a bluff, and they were made of logs and canvas. The shelters were nothing fancy yet if a lot of bush existed, we'd build a log shack. They were small places because all you needed was a bed and a stove in the corner. It was never a problem if we met at a shelter together, the only thing was one of us had to sleep on the floor. Between us we set down around 800 traps.

I never traveled in a hurry. When I made a trapline, I liked to put four traps to a mile and Fredie and I both trapped in different directions, not just in a straight line. I would travel along until I saw a nice spot—if a tree was close I'd tie the trap to it. If not, I'd build a snow mound and anchor the trap to a stick in the mound. The mound I'd make would be about two feet high. In the centre of the mound I'd place the trap then cover it with a snow pan. To make a snow pan you'd cut a block of snow with a snow knife, put it over the trap, then shave it down—shave it down to nothing. You can see the outline of the trap through it and the beauty of a mound is that it seldom ever blows in. Afterwards I'd sprinkle chopped up bait around the mound. Some years were lean. Fredie and I had a year when we didn't make enough money to buy groceries but we also had a year when we made $11,000, and $11,000 in those days was a lot of money. Butter during that year was $.40 a pound. The best hunt we ever made was 400 foxes with some selling as high as $40.

The fox run came during the months of November and December. You had to work like the dickens to get the fur before Christmas because after that you may as well stay home and sleep. We always skinned our foxes right away, and then we'd roll them up and let them freeze. In January and February, after everything quieted down, we'd stretch and clean our catch. For two months you went non-stop, and we never did stop. After the foxes moved north in January and February, nothing seemed to move. It was too cold to move!

Sometimes the weather was cold during these years—very cold. We don't get the cold, the bitter cold, now like we did then. Sometimes a whiteout could last for four days. The climate has changed since then. It's warmer now. I used to listen to the radio and you'd hear it said that the temperature was –60 degrees F, that's what I call a bitter cold and since I've left that area and moved to Churchill, I've never seen the cold again.

During one snowstorm, we almost lost Ilse, one of my sisters who we took back up with us one year. Well, it was a nice enough morning that day and then a storm came up around noon. I guess Fredie and her could have stayed at one of our camps but they decided to move on. He should have stayed because they had to travel through an open area and when they went through, they somehow got separated. She was lost in a whiteout for four days. It was no problem for him to survive but she wandered around for five more days. She was lucky to find a camp. She was very lucky. The camp belonged to Ragnar Jonsson and he found her after the storm and brought her seventy-five miles back to our cabin. The storm was bad, and "yes" she was lucky to survive!

Christmas day wasn't a special occasion to us. It was the same as any other day outside of the fact that we knew it was Christmas. All that we did was stay home. There were no presents or anything. You see, we had a day-to-day life with few family traditions. My father always handled the money and he was good to us. When it came to any kind of clothing, camping gear, toboggans, or rifles, we got them so there was no need for exchanging gifts. Dad trapped for a while but in the later years, he mostly stayed at home. Like I said, he did all the cooking and when Fredie and I trapped, Dad always had everything ready to go. He made bread, doughnuts, and when he made hamburgers he'd make two hundred at a time, that way our grub box was always full. There was no need for extra giving on Christmas; we gave to one another all year round.

After Christmas I'd take off traveling around the country up there. We had lots of time on our hands so I'd travel just to see what's over the next hill. One year I took a notion to go to Dubuant Lake because I had a good team. You never ran into a lot of people but that was when I first ran into Frits Oftedal. He was up around the Padlei country looking for caribou. I remember meeting him because after we made camp and were frying up meat, I passed him my onion salt. I told him what it was but he never believed me, when he sprinkled some on the caribou and said, "Holy smokes, it does smell like onion!" It was the little things like that, that made meeting people so much fun. That was the first year I remember onion and garlic salts coming out and Dad had bought a bunch of cartons (they came twelve to a carton).

Up north it never mattered what time of day it was, where you were, or where you were going when you met someone. We lived by the rule of thumb that you stopped right there and made camp. We weren't a people to just shake hands and say bye, bye. We always pulled into the nearest bush and made camp. It didn't matter what the person was—white, Chipewyan, or Inuit. You'd enjoy an evening together, even in sign language, then part ways in the morning.

It wasn't hard for people to live up there. The clothing we wore weighed very little. Today if I go hunting, I need about twenty pounds of clothes to keep warm on the skidoo. Back then I would go to the nearest Eskimo camp to buy clothes.

I'd get a parka for two or three pounds of tea, and my caribou parka never weighed more than two pounds. My whole outfit up north never weighed over five or six pounds.

We had good sleighs. We used trees for runners. Sometimes you would have to split the tree for a runner, sometimes not. I found tamarack to be the best. Once the tamarack is cut down, then split in half, it slips real nice. Mud runners I didn't care for, as they were hard to use. The problem was that once you hit a bump or rock, a chunk would fall off. To make a mud runner is quite easy. You go back into the muskeg and get a chunk of peat bog and break it down. You chop it up and mix it something like baking bread, kind of doughy. Then apply it to the runners of your sleigh. After you apply it to the runners, you let it freeze, then plane it over with a runner plane. The smoother you make it when you apply it, the less planing you do. Then all you do is ice them; that is, add water, let it freeze, then plane it again. That's my mud runner recipe!

During our years up there, we ran into most of the different animals that lived inland up north. For years, we never saw any polar bears, then one year they came through. Polar bears never belonged inland, they belonged on the coast. Where we lived the area was half tundra and half bush. In the winter you could walk anywhere. Twenty miles north of us was almost true tundra, however, there were still little bushes and bluffs. Anyway, the polar bears sure made a mess. They got into our meat caches and everything, but after that year they never came through again.

Another year the magpies came through. Imagine that! Magpies! I don't know where they came from. Then another year the porcupines came in thick. After that, black bears. I imagine it depended on the animal population down south to push them north.

We had trouble with wolves, generally in the winter. They would bother our traplines and once they start following your line, they are a nuisance. Oh, we'd set some traps for them but how we really got rid of them; I don't care to mention. We just got rid of them, that's all!

Wolverines weren't a problem. He's a curious animal and a real pest. Ragnar Jonsson, a white trapper, taught me how to trap them. You need a big trap because the wolverine is heavy for his size and has big feet that act like snowshoes. The best bait was a skinned fox carcass. One time my brother had one following his line, stealing all his foxes and he couldn't get rid of it. That wolverine used to turn all the traps upside down so it didn't matter if they tripped or not. Anyway, we found a dead caribou that a wolf had killed and the wolverine was hanging around it, so we set a double barrel shotgun trap to a fox carcass beside the caribou. Well, the wolverine pulled on the fox and caught both barrels. You know, that wolverine had three toes missing on his left front foot so someone had caught him before. You read all these stories about wolverines and people have it in their minds that he's like the devil or something. Well, he's not! He's just an animal, very stupid, and very smelly, too!

The country we lived in was caribou country. The caribou weren't there by the thousands; they were there by the hundreds of thousands. I don't know what's happened over the years, but the country's empty now. I thought the caribou would've made a comeback by now but no, they didn't. Inland in those days, the people killed a lot of caribou and there were still a lot left. Even today, with the Eskimos having been placed in villages and hamlets along the coast, the caribou are still scarce. A lot of caribou were killed in those days, in a sense, too damn many! Don't forget though, in the olden days a lot were killed but a lot existed. Even in Churchill years ago, the caribou migrated through but now there's nothing. My father used to say to me, "Look now, you'll never see it again!" He was right. All those caribou would move and we'd sit and watch them. It used to take three weeks for the caribou to move north and all of that to move south. Each year the migrations were pretty much the same. When they moved north, we only took (shot) a few, not like some of the natives who killed them just for the sake of killing! Come September, Pop would say, "It's time to go and shoot our meat for the winter." Gee, there were some nice big bucks and they'd have up to three inches of fat on them. But come the winter, they sure got skinny. By September 20, the rut would be on so we wouldn't bother them anymore.

When we put up our meat caches, we'd wait as long as possible until the weather was cool. You'd shoot your caribou, gut him, then turn him over on his belly with his legs apart and leave him. Once he's cooled, you'd bring him home. You could look at the hills and there were caribou everywhere, then in a week, maybe two, a storm would come up and the next morning when you got up, nothing! The caribou were all passed, headed for the bush. I was raised on caribou meat, and I sure liked it.

You know how most people like steaks; well the Eskimos never cared for them. They'd grab the hindquarters of a caribou and chop them up for the dogs. What was left, say ½ inch of meat around the bone, they'd crack up and throw it into a pot. They'd do the same with the ribs and brisket. They never fried a steak like we did. In a way, it's meat abuse but I've seen worse, much worse. I've seen both sides of the shore so stinking you couldn't camp there. They used to go in August to kill caribou for their skins. Oh, they'd take the hides, cut the tongue out, and maybe some briskets and ribs, but the rest they left—to rot. Once we paddled down a river for two miles and all we saw was dead caribou on both sides. My brother Fredie said, "Oh my gosh, I'm going to get sick!" Stink! You never smelled the likes of it. They took the hides, their favorite meat, and left them. That's the Inuit who did this.

The Chipewyans were no better. They often killed just for what appeared to be the sake of killing. The Chipewyans who came from the Duck Lake area were good tanners though. We used to get tanned hides from them. You could buy a tanned hide for $2.00. They tanned using caribou brains and their skins were nice and white.

We fed our dogs mostly fish but sometimes caribou meat. We put up quite a few animals in the fall but never more than we needed and we never went hungry. We never killed like the Eskimo did. We'd do our hunt while in the meantime the Eskimo along the river would kill 1000! They never hunted, they slaughtered. They'd kill and kill and kill. When they'd stop and it was time to clean them, a man might say, "This caribou doesn't look so good." So he'd cut the tongue out and leave the rest. If it didn't look so good, he shouldn't have shot it. He had eyes, too, you know. The truth is that a lot of abuse did exist.

In the old days, the Eskimo camps weren't much. They moved around a lot, as they didn't have any permanent camps. One time they'd be one place then the next time you came along, they'd be ten miles away. It all depended on where they shot their meat. We generally went to their camps just to visit or to buy clothes.

The better hunters had the better camps, and I traded with them for clothing. They made your clothing on the spot—boots, parka, whatever you wanted and I bought my clothes with tea, or tobacco, sometimes coffee. Those items were our money up north.

The Inland Eskimos where we were never had a true igloo. They had snow walls with posts across the top covered with skins for a roof. Their homes were actually quite large and they used their stove only to boil tea or cook meat, not really for heat. It seems to me the first few years when I was up there, the people weren't starving but after the sickness came, the people changed.

There were always a lot of caribou so I don't see how the people could have been weaker. In later years I think their fault was that they didn't prepare enough. In a sense they went from one extreme to another and I think they weren't a people to think too far ahead into the future. They could have prepared a lot of dried meat to keep on hand like we did. It's hard to understand.

I recall the Eskimos trading a lot of fur some years. I wouldn't say they were rich or anything. Most of the time they appeared to be pretty hard up. It's like anything else; there were both good and poor trappers and hunters amongst the Eskimo. Poverty existed among them, especially with the lazy ones who wouldn't move around and work at life. An Eskimo who would have moved around and worked at hunting and trapping could have lived like a king the years I was up there. We always had some of the lazy ones hanging around the Post or the house.

I know one thing for sure; the father was the boss. What he said went! The Eskimos were a people of their own with the caribou their main diet. They did fish a little, mainly when they had to, but I don't think they cared to eat fish all that much.

I know that Shamanism existed. Shamanism is true but I never saw it practiced. Oh, you'd see someone walking around with fancy extras on, so something must have happened. My father called them Medicine Men and all the Shamans I ever saw were men, although there apparently were two women Shamans living east of us. Regarding the Shamans, my father told us, "Don't you ever let them outdo you—outdo them a little bit and be friends with them, then they'll be friends with you!" By golly, he was right.

During the days we were up there, drinking didn't exist and I'm sure the Eskimos never knew what drinking was. I can't really place my finger on what it was to start the Eskimos to go downhill but they did.

When I found Rita, a young Eskimo girl, in one of their camps, the people were already hungry and starving. I didn't know that 'til I went their way to look for clothing. I found Rita all alone at one camp and when I went on to the next camp, there they were—starving. I had put up a lot of caribou that fall and as far as I know, there were plenty around, but somehow they didn't get enough. Probably they ran short of ammunition because when I found them, they had nothing.

I told them all to pack up and follow me to one of my camps on the Kazan River. I took them there and gave them all the meat I had. They didn't even have dogs by then—their dogs had starved to death! Yes, it was a pitiful sight. There we were with twenty-five miles to travel but we made it to my camp walking and pushing sleighs. When we got to the cabin, I left them and headed home. The next time I came back up, they were short of meat again so I took them to another camp, which was the only thing to do. They hung around there for quite a while and I was able to spare them some shells. The first time I didn't think to send a message south for help, but the second time I managed to get a message out.

The first year the government helped them the best they could but up north the government always seemed to be too late. The government should have come in there two years sooner but that's hindsight. The government, of course, did the wrong thing first and moved them to Padlei, into the bush country. The bush country of all places! That sure didn't help very much. Why didn't the government leave them right where they were, on their home ground? That way they would at least have known what to do. All that the people would have needed to get back on their feet was ammunition and dogs. Now these people are finally settled in towns and hamlets along the coast. Maybe the caribou did miss the

Inuit camps but if they did, it had to be in their part of the country. They never missed in our area because all the time I was there, the caribou came through and usually at the same time of year.

The Eskimos were dying before we left the country and I heard a lot more died after we left. I'll always remember one Eskimo from that country. His name was Ohoto. I guess he broke into the store around Padlei because he was starving so they moved him to Eskimo Point where they were building a town for the Eskimos. Well, they put him in jail for a spell and while he was in, they sent him down to the beach to break rock with a sledgehammer. I don't think much of the R.C.M.P. for doing a thing like that. He was pounding a hammer when pieces of rocks flew into his eyes. He went blind, total blindness in both eyes. That R.C.M.P. officer must have hated him to make a man do such nonsense. Ohoto could have done a lot of other things like clean the yard, or paint the buildings, or even sweep the floor. Another R.C.M.P. officer told me of this incident and we were both very saddened by it.

The Eskimos were afraid of the R.C.M.P. and with good reason. They had a fear of being taken away.

We used to have R.C.M.P. visits once a year when we first went to Windy River and if someone spoke of thievery I'd call him a liar. We never had thievery when I was there and no one ever locked a door. Your house door was always left open, wide open, and your house was available for anyone to use. I really don't have fond thoughts of the R.C.M.P. I remember my dad telling them, "I'd sure like to send my kids to school," and they more or less just laughed. Nowadays, if you're up north and your kids don't go to school, the R.C.M.P. will fly in and make sure your kids get to school.

I remember when Francis Harper came in and stayed at my cabin. He was very well educated—a biologist. He came in the spring to catch birds and bugs. We got along very well. He and Farley Mowat came together but they didn't get along very well. Farley Mowat was okay in a way, but to me he just took care of himself. He was doing a similar work to Francis Harper. I felt sorry for Francis. He had sugar diabetes and every morning he'd have to shoot himself with the needle.

They came in April of 1947. Later, Farley Mowat wanted to get out so I took him out. Mowat paid me to take him out and after I got back to Nueltin Lake, he wrote me a letter stating that he wanted his money back. I guess he was broke in those days. When I think of Farley Mowat, well, I don't want to say too much. Why bother, he knows! He was a person who never said "thank-you." Just jumped on the plane and took off. He's a good writer in a way, for people who don't know him.

From 1937 to the time we left, in 1948, I was never really affected by the changes that took place up north. You see, we changed with the times and we were never hungry. If I wanted fish, I'd set a net; there were always a lot of fish in the river. The biggest change came with the caribou, the animals thinned out, however, some were still in the area. The years up north were "good, too good." It was nice up north. Now Fredie tells me, "Remember, it was so peaceful and quiet up there!" We had money, you know, but the most important thing we had was a caribou roast and I never have it here anymore.

We left because the price of fur fell. The last year we shipped our fur to Winnipeg and the buyers even had trouble selling it. There was nothing to stay for. We and the Eskimos ended up with nothing. The last few years we couldn't even take trade goods in. No one wanted anything to do with trading. Even if the foxes would have been tripping over each other to get in the traps, your reds only brought $.75 each, so you may as well have left them live. The war had kept the price of fur up, but when it ended, the prices started to fall.

There were a lot of good times up north. Some of the fellows, the other trappers, had a girlfriend or two and when the market fell out, you could say a few wives got left behind. When I was in Baker Lake in 1981, I'd look at a few people and smile to myself. You can't go up north and get a wife or a woman like in the old days. Then you just had to approach the husband, but I'm proud to say I never left any kids behind. We weren't raised like that.

Since I left Churchill I've worked for the government, except when in Atikokan, Ontario, Winnipeg, Prince Albert, Saskatchewan, and Fort Nelson, British Columbia. When I came back to Churchill, I went back with the government. I was married twenty-five years ago and my wife and I have had seven boys and one girl. As well, there were two other kids, Irene and Alfred, you could say we adopted.

I only have good thoughts of the old days up north. I wish I could do it all again.

◆◆◆

"The Eskimos of the Kazan River were fortunate to have a man of Charlie's caliber in their country with them during the years the foxes ran."

Gerry Dunning

The End of the Trail

I have often wondered why people such as ourselves sometimes become so hooked on the North. Now, I think I know. In canoeing strange and little known river systems including crossings from one headwater to another where no trails exist, one is often facing and overcoming the forces of nature. Then there are the worries that may accompany these activities as you travel through the deep wilderness as we do, without ever packing a firearm.

Gusty and adverse winds while crossing the larger lakes, insect problems beyond description, severe thunderstorms blowing the tent down during night-time downpours or rain as lightning flashes nearby, are only a few of the forces of nature wilderness paddlers in the North may have to overcome. Good judgment in reading a river where quick and correct decisions must be made as to whether to get ashore to look it over, or to shoot on into a drop in the river is also a part of it. Indeed, it is a memorable experience to find yourself in the midst of the wilderness, hundreds of miles from civilization and realize that your return depends only on the efforts of you and your partner.

Some call it a disease known as Arctic Fever when one wants to go North time after time. It is easy to become bitten by the "spell of the North." People who have smelled the smoke of a campfire and inhaled the pure forest air laden with the smell of spruce, or on a cold day have sipped a cup of hot Labrador tea, or dipped their paddles into untamed waters will know what this means. The fever of exploration gets into one's blood and draws a person back to those wild rivers and forests of the North time after time in spite of one's resolutions to go no more. Yes, there is something about it that each time you return home, you will soon hear the voice of the wilderness calling you to return one more time. This feeling can best be described by a verse from ***Spell of the Yukon*** by Robert W. Service:

The summer—no sweeter was ever;
The sunshiny woods all athrill;
The grayling aleap in the river,
The bighorn asleep on the hill.
The strong life that never knows harness;
The wilds where the caribou call;
The freshness, the freedom, the farness—
O God! How I'm stuck on it all.

While working our way through the Nunavut wilderness in 2001 it became apparent that I no longer had the stamina or physical power to plan or attempt another such journey in the future. It was time to hang up my paddle. Consequently, with fond memories of our 7,500 plus miles of canoeing North of 60, I compose these poems:

The Paddling Octogenarian

Soon after the spring breakup of ice on the lakes,
Heading north of 60 is just what it takes
    To make ourselves happy!
Those extra hours of sunshine are a wonderful thing
To make an old guy happy and feel like a king.

The people down home think we are out of our mind
To come way up here just to see what we can find.
    We like to explore!
It's a continuing problem but each summer we go forth,
while the folks at home wonder why we're so hooked on the North.

One trip across the portage with the heaviest packs.
Then we do an about face and tote the remaining sacks
    But that isn't all—
Next time it's the canoes. Can we make it ahead of the rain?
Sure! Rain is great sport, if you're conditioned against all pain.

It's those rivers and creeks we just have to explore.
We wonder what's around the next bend. There's even more,
    Have your camera ready—
It could be an animal, maybe a wolf, bear or moose
We quietly approach. Scenery's great. This time, it's only a goose!

There's much more to our story. Soon we enter a big lake
Wind's in our favor. Camping time has arrived, so a fish we take
    We're tired and hungry.
We paddle to esker, set up tents and blow up air mattress
Octogenarian crawls in for a snooze to relieve all the stress.

While son cleans the fish, then the supper he preps
As the old paddler snores, then into moccasins he slips.
    Why not be comfortable?
Lots of black flies and bulldogs. Soon the mosquitoes appear.
Finally supper is ready. Now it's time for some cheer!

But as supper is served, more mosquitoes move in
We know what they want. It's a piece of our skin.
    They're hungry, too!
On to our plates they swarm getting stuck in the food
So rapid we eat, mosquitoes and all. Gee! They taste good.

Nowadays it's hard to keep up, but I certainly try
To match my partner step-for-step and he may wonder why,
    As so often I sigh.
Slowly I now wobble along doing the best that I can
To keep pace with our son. He's indeed quite a man.

He comes back to help me get up whenever I fall.
He's willing to assist at any time I may call—
    He seems happy to help.
I'm a fortunate old paddler. That's perfectly clear
To have had such a great partner for so many a year.

The paddling octogenarian is what they called me.
There were so many more rivers I still wanted to see
    And all of those lakes?
But time has now run out for me with paddle and pack
Now I'm much more comfortable at home, lying flat on my back.

The Urge of the Octogenarian

Night times in sleeping bags are things to enjoy
After a hard day's work with paddle and pack
    I've an ache in my back
Now it's time for some rest for this good old boy
So with aching arms, shoulders and back, I zip up my sack.

Yes. Night times in a tent is definitely a thing I enjoy
Snuggled down in my sack is indeed a great joy
    It's just so comfortable!
Two or three hours and I awake with the urge
To unzip the tent—to get out and splurge!

But that isn't so easy for me anymore
First I unzip my bag—then reach for tent door
    The pressure is building!
I roll over on elbows and knees and crawl to the fly
This time there's no cramp in my leg and I wonder why?

Bare except for my shorts and hat, I wobble to my feet
Step out on a carpet of caribou moss, I thought was so neat
    Really gotta go!!!
The east wind is blowing from across the lake
I turn facing downwind. Now I'm ready to make.

So I concentrate on the priming. Those mosquitoes have moved in
A swing of the hat across legs, shoulders and back—now it's prime again
    Must ignore those bugs.
Finally sweet relief. But the swarm has arrived. I crawl back into tent
Zip it up quickly and brush off my feet. Now my energy's all spent.

Hundreds of mosquitoes have followed me in. With my feet in the bag
I reach for the Raid, cover my face with my hat, now those pests can't nag
    Oh! I'm comfortable again.
But it doesn't last long. Less than two hours later this maneuver I repeat.
Guess it comes with ripe old age. It's really a treat to again fall asleep.

Then another hour or two as loons whimper from across the lake
Thunder rumbles as a cold wind picks up causing the tent to shake
    Oh! No! I've gotta go again!!!
I grab my old Tilley, crawling out as fast as I can
I make it to my feet. Lightning flashes! And there I stand.

Now to concentrate on the prime as raindrops begin to fly
It must be done quickly so harder I try. Oh! My-My!
    I'm going to get wet!
My old hat brim's not wide enough to keep me dry
Soon soaked to the skin. I stand there for one final try.

"Breakfast's almost ready." The next thing I hear is my partner's call.
"It's time to get up, Dad. Weather looks great. Let's get on the ball!"
    I crawl out to enjoy another day.
Before coffee is poured the octogenarian wobbles behind big spruce
Then he returns to face another day and to lace up his boots.

Bibliography

Browning, Peter. ***The Last Wilderness.*** Lafayette, CA: Chronicle Books, 1975.

Downes, P.G. ***Sleeping Island***. Saskatoon, Saskatchewan: Western Producer Prairie Books, 1988.

Dunning, Gerry. ***When the Foxes Ran***. Churchill, Manitoba: Gerry Dunning, 1996.

Harper, Francis. ***Caribou Eskimos of the Upper Kazan River***. Lawrence, KS: University of Kansas, 1964.

Hodgins, W. Bruce and Gweneth Hoyle. ***Canoeing North Into the Unknown.*** Peterborough, Ontario: Natural Heritage, 1994.

Keighley, Sydney Augustus. ***Trader • Tripper • Trapper.*** Winnipeg, Manitoba: University of Winnipeg, 1989.

Kemp, H.S.M. ***Northern Trader***. Toronto, Ontario: Ryerson Press, 1956.

Lowery, Bob. ***The Unbeatable Breed***. Winnipeg, Manitoba: The Prairie Publishing Co., 1981.

Mowat, Farley. ***The People of the Deer***. Boston, MA: Little Brown and Company, 1952.

Olson, Sigurd F. ***The Lonely Land.*** New York, NY: Alfred A. Knopf, 1966.

Pettigrew, R. King. ***North of Stony Rapids***. Victoria, British Columbia: R. King Pettigrew, 1989.

Index

About the Author

This avid explorer has paddled and portaged more than 7500 miles of Canada's Arctic and Subarctic waterways. An active outdoorsman, he has walked more than 40,000 miles during the past 34 years.

Clayton founded Klein Fertilizer Company in 1951 and operated it for 30 years before turning the management over to his son. Finding retirement too quiet, he started Wilderness Adventure Books, a publishing company specializing in Great Lakes titles. After retiring from publishing in 1992, he founded Klein's Booklein, a wholesale book business serving the Great Lakes.

He lives on a farm near Fowlerville, Michigan, in the house in which he was born. When he's not busy walking and canoeing, Clate keeps busy writing, learning how to operate a computer, and tending his garden, fruit trees, and yard.